TOMORROW
AT DAWN!

Also by J. G. de Beus

The Rebirth of the Kingdom and six reprints by the Dutch underground
press

The Future of the West (translated and published in thirteen languages)

J. G. de Beus

TOMORROW
AT DAWN!

W·W·NORTON & COMPANY·*NEW YORK*·*LONDON*

First Edition

Library of Congress Cataloging in Publication Data
Beus, Jacobus Gijsbertus de, 1909–
   Tomorrow at dawn!
   Bibliography: p.
   Includes index.
      1. World War, 1939–1945—Germany. 2. World War, 1939–1945—Per-
sonal narratives, Dutch. 3. Beus, Jacobus Gijsbertus de, 1909–   4. World
War, 1939–1945—Campaigns—Western. 5. Sas, Gijsbert J. 6. Oster, Hans.
7. Treason—Germany. 8. Germany—History—1933–1945. I. Title.
D757.B46 1979   940.54'21   79–18228

ISBN 0–393–01263–8

1 2 3 4 5 6 7 8 9 0

To Louise
without whose constant assistance this book
would never have come into being

CONTENTS

Preface   9

ONE   August 1939: The Dance on the Volcano   13

TWO   Fall Weiss   33

THREE   Enter the Ghost Informer   43

FOUR   The November Alarm   53
Twelve minutes that could have saved the world • The Venlo incident • The catastrophe that did not happen

FIVE   The Winter of Nerves   70
The alarm of January 1940

SIX   *Weser Exercise*   95
The warning to Norway • The warning to Denmark: "Nonsense! Nonsense!" • The warning to England

SEVEN   The Last Act: May 1940   119
The first day • The second day • The third day • The fourth day • The fifth day • The sixth day • The seventh day

EIGHT   The Eve of War   138
Another last supper of peace • The ultimatum

NINE   Aftermath   153
Farewell to Sas: cocktails with bombs

8   *Contents*

TEN The Invisible Informer   169
The eagle's last flight

Bibliography   181

Index   185

PREFACE

THIS BOOK TELLS an incredible story. During the first eight months of World War II a high German officer in a key position consistently provided the Netherlands Military Attaché in Berlin with detailed information about Hitler's plans for attack on the Western front. These urgent messages were skeptically received by the governments concerned, so that these very governments were taken by surprise by the sudden occupation of Denmark and Norway in April 1940 and by the big offensive against the Netherlands, Belgium, Luxemburg, and France on May 10, 1940.

Although this is a spy story in one sense—recalling the well-known Cicero story—the secret informer in this case was not a spy for personal gain, but a German patriot who acted from moral indignation about Hitler's regime and methods. The informer was convinced that the offensive in the West would bring disaster not only to the neutral countries attacked and to Europe as a whole, but above all to Germany itself. He paid with his life for trying to prevent it.

The numerous warnings sent by the Netherlands Legation in Berlin between the end of the Polish campaign and the offensive in the West were all destroyed in May 1940, but the author, then Secretary of the Netherlands Legation in Berlin, has been able to reconstruct them all. His sources include his own experience and notes as well as the postwar testimony of Major G. J. Sas, the Netherlands Military Attaché who had contact with the informer, and the information Sas always simultaneously provided to the Belgian Military Attaché, whose dispatches escaped destruction. The author is extremely grateful to Monsieur Jean van Welkenhuyzen, Director of the Belgian Research Center for the History of World War II, for having made these available; they were immensely valuable in reconstructing Major Sas' warnings. Since the original texts of these warnings no longer exist, the author cannot vouch for the literal correctness of the reconstructed cyphers, but he *can* vouch for their correctness in date and substance.

Some thirty years after the distressing experiences related in this book, the author was appointed Netherlands Ambassador to the Federal Republic of Germany. He is extremely thankful that his seven years' service in the new Germany have shown him that the country which under Hitler constituted the greatest source of unrest is now, as a parliamentary democracy, one of the main pillars of the stability, security, and unprecedented prosperity Europe has enjoyed for over thirty years.

J. G. DE BEUS

Note: The contents of this book are exclusively the personal responsibility of the author and do not represent any government or official views.

TOMORROW AT DAWN!

One

AUGUST 1939: THE DANCE ON THE VOLCANO

BERLIN WAS STIFLING in the summer of 1939. And we in the Netherlands Legation were convinced that it would be even hotter before we reached the safe haven of the Nazi *Parteitag des Friedens*—*if* we reached it. This "Party Convention of Peace" was scheduled for the second week of September, undoubtedly to celebrate another "peaceful" Nazi victory. As he had done the year before, after the infamous Munich agreement, Hitler would announce to tens of thousands of madly cheering followers and to a resentful but relieved world that he had again preserved peace by swallowing part of a neighboring country and a few million of its inhabitants. We had seen this performance all too often, sometimes live in Berlin, sometimes in the films of party conventions in Nuremberg.

We had no doubt that August 1939 would decide the question of war or peace and might therefore be as fateful in world history as August 1914, twenty-five years earlier. By objective standards, the risk of war was clearly even greater now than it had been in 1914.

Then the Great Powers had "slithered into war," as a German statesman put it; the Austrian, Russian, and German Empires had tried to bully their opponents into political concessions by ultimatums and military threats. They had taken irresponsible risks and miscalculated. Even so, none had deliberately aimed for war.

But now? For six years Europe had lived from crisis to crisis, each following more quickly and each more dangerous than the last, and always caused by the same demonic power: Hitler's national socialism.

Often during the summer of 1939 we foreign diplomats in Berlin reviewed the crises through which we had lived since January 30, 1933, when internal weaknesses finally brought down the parliamentary system of the Weimar Republic and Hitler seized power. That evening, when he stood at the floodlit window of the *Reichs-kanzlei*, the seat of German government, hysterically cheered by thousands of supporters, he could with some justification tell his followers that a new era had begun: "the greatest revolution of world history, the revolution of the Germanic race against non-Aryans, Mongols, Bolsheviks, and liberals." He had taken firm possession of power in Germany. Equally firm was his determination to possess Europe.

Europe held its breath. It still refused to believe that Hitler would carry out the sweeping and aggressive program described in his book *Mein Kampf*. This program included recovering all the teritories lost in 1919 to Poland and Lithuania, as well as the Saarland, lost to France; bringing about the *Anschluss,* the union of Germany with Austria; and annexing the Sudetenland, the Czech frontier areas populated by the Sudeten Germans. Then would come a knockout blow to France, not for its own sake but to safeguard Germany's rear as it attacked to the East, claiming the fertile fields of Poland and the Ukraine to meet its supposed need for "Lebensraum," living space. The whole of this astounding program was spelled out clearly in *Mein Kampf.* Yet outside Germany very few believed that Hitler would actually carry it out in practice; it seemed too daring, too fantastic, too irresponsible. Then, step by step, it happened.

Even in Holland, where public opinion had always resented the rising national socialism next door, many believed that once Hitler was established in power he would not practice all he had preached. But he did.

The members of the Dutch Legation in Berlin (Holland did not yet have Embassies then) were far more pessimistic about Hitler than our government or public opinion at home. Other Western diplomats in Berlin felt the same. Every day we saw the symptoms of preparation for war—troops marching by, the economy being geared for self-sufficiency, the dwindling supplies of imported consumer goods, luxury items, food, and gasoline. A small example illustrates both the mood and the scarcity of goods in those days. Because we might soon have to pack all our belongings, we went out to buy a steamer trunk. The salesman could produce only one, which he strongly advised us to buy: it was his last one, and, he whispered confidentially, it was American made, therefore sturdier than a German-made trunk. He was right: I still use it forty years later.

Even more telling than the determined striving for economic self-sufficiency was the ruthlessness of the Nazi system, its cruelty to the Jews—crowds of whom filled the Legation waiting room every day, trying to obtain Dutch visas—and its disdain for all people who did not belong to the master race of Aryan and Germanic blood. Equally disgusting was the spying and denouncing carried out even in society circles by the few who were not, like most in these circles, anti-Nazi. This atmosphere of fear gave rise to the "Berliner Blick," a quick look over the shoulder before criticizing the regime. Diplomats stationed in Berlin, witnessing these elements of daily life, believed the Nazis far more capable of ruthless deeds than did the government and public opinion at home. There, people resented the Nazi regime, but not as emotionally as those who experienced it twenty-four hours a day.

This powerful resentment was shared by almost all members of our Legation, from relative newcomers like the Minister, Jonkheer van Haersma de With, just arrived from Washington, and myself, just arrived from Copenhagen, to old hands like the Chancellor, the secretaries, and our faithful German doorman.

I say *almost* all members, because one or two unreliable elements had managed to push their way in. One was the new young German assistant doorman, taken on because of the flood of Jewish visitors applying for visas. He was diligent and eager to please—maybe somewhat too eager, and we had the impression that he was trying somewhat too often to listen at doors and to tidy up papers during one's absence.

The other was a beautiful girl, sent as a secretary from The Hague to cope with the flood of visa applications. She was easy on the eye, but when we checked her background we were shocked to find that she belonged to the small Dutch Nazi party. We immediately requested her recall, but her appointment was indicative of the naiveté and inadequacy of our security.

Hitler's surprise moves usually took place in early spring, around the middle of March. Another surprise sometimes followed in late summer, to be exuberantly celebrated by a huge party convention in September.

The world did not have to wait long for its first unpleasant surprise. On October 14, 1933, less than a yer after coming to power, Hitler announced his astonishing decision to leave the Disarmament Conference and the League of Nations. Secretly he ordered armed resistance if sanctions were applied against Germany. This proved unnecessary. As would so often happen, Hitler had correctly estimated how much affront he could give without incurring effective retaliation.

He was equally successful in his attempt to bring about the hotly debated and strongly opposed merger of Austria with Germany. In July 1934 Austrian Nazis even murdered their own "little Chancellor," Dollfuss, who opposed the *Anschluss*, but their coup failed and Hitler promptly disavowed all complicity.

In mid-March 1935 Hitler announced Germany's rearmament and demonstrated it by the first massive military review of the reborn German army.

A year later—again around the middle of March and again during a weekend—Hitler occupied the demilitarized Rhineland, knowing full well that under the provisions of the 1919 peace treaty this would constitute a *casus belli.* "If the French had then moved in," he was to declare later, "I would have had to withdraw ignominiously." But again he had gambled and won.

Two years later, after several more thwarted attempts to bring about the *Anschluss* of Austria with Germany, Hitler engineered the Austrian Chancellor's ouster from office and an invitation to Germany from the Austrian usurpers "to come to the aid of the Austrian nation." On March 12, 1938, Nazi tanks thundered into Austria, decked out in flowers and welcomed by wildly cheering crowds. On the main square of Vienna Hitler announced Austria's entry into the German Reich.

Europe had only a few months to catch its breath before Hitler started a political and propaganda campaign against Czechoslovakia. With diabolic genius Goebbels' propaganda machine began to agitate against the unbearable fate of the Sudeten Germans, a German minority living just inside the borders of Czechoslovakia. Again the Western democracies had neither the nerve nor the determination to stand up to Hitler's unscrupulous aggressiveness. On September 29, 1938, under the threat of a German invasion, the infamous Munich agreement was signed, forcing Czechoslovakia to give up the Sudeten German areas, and with them its border defenses—an all-time low of shame and appeasement. The Western powers signed with deep frustration and equally deep relief.

Hitler had announced that the Sudetenland would be his last territorial claim, but the ink of his signature had hardly dried when on October 21 he ordered plans to be drawn up for occupying the rest of Czechoslovakia and for annexing the Memelland, the border area Germany had lost to Lithuania in 1919. Six months later, on March 15, 1939, at 6 A.M.—again on the Ides of March and again at dawn—German forces occupied the defenseless remnant of Czechoslovakia. Tht same month Hitler forced Lithuania to cede the Memelland.

At the height of the Sudeten crisis, when it became obvious that Czechoslovakia had lost, Poland entered the conflict and successfully claimed the territory of Teschen in Upper Silesia, which had been ceded to Czechoslovakia at the end of World War I. I remember a British colleague's biting remark, characteristic of the mood of those days: "The Poles will be next at it—and I shall not be sorry for them!"

Indeed, after the annexation of the Sudetenland and the Memelland there were no obstacles to the next object of Hitler's insatiable drive for expansion: the return to the Reich of the "Free City of Danzig," created in 1919 as a neutral territory uder the control of the League of Nations. He likewise demanded free transit rights through the Polish Corridor, which since 1919 had separated East Prussia from the rest of Germany.

But at last the Western democracies had learned

their lesson. Poland rejected the German demands outright, and ten days later Britain gave Poland a security guarantee that was immediately and vociferously denounced by Nazi propaganda as a "blank check."

Now that a major Western power had committed itself to oppose Hitler, all events led to war with the inevitability of a Greek tragedy. On the diplomatic grandstand in Berlin we watched powerlessly as the catastrophe approached.

At the end of April 1939 Hitler, in one of his most aggressive speeches, cancelled both the naval armament agreement with England and the treaty of friendship with Poland. As we listened to his invective, interspersed with thunderous applause, we all had the ominous impression that the die was cast: Hitler had decided to force the issue.

In fact, on April 3 he had already instructed the *Oberkommando der Wehrmacht,* the Supreme Command of the Armed Forces, to draw up plans for "Fall Weiss," the war against Poland. In a secret explanation to his military commanders at the end of May, he emphasized that fundamentally his aim was not Danzig, but a much wider one: "Lebensraum," living space for Germany in the East. "Let no one think," he shouted, "that the events of Czechoslovakia are going to be repeated! This time it is going to be war!" In June he ordered all preparations to be completed by August 20.

All these decisions were, of course, made in deepest secrecy; none of the diplomats in Berlin knew about them. But even so the shape of things to come began to take an ever clearer and more threatening form. In addition our Military Attaché, Major Gijsbert Sas, was already reaping the fruits of an old friendship with a German colleague which would be of inestimable value in the coming months. This German officer had informed Sas of orders that had been given for full preparedness by early August for war with Poland.

When we evaluated this information against the background of the last few years, we had little doubt that the late summer of 1939 would produce a crisis even deeper than the previous ones. We foresaw an awful prospect: either the West again on its knees to avoid war, or Armageddon let loose over Europe. And once the Polish crisis had peaked, it seemed highly unlikely that Hitler would refrain from carrying out his plans to dominate the whole continent.

Our forebodings were expressed on June 22, 1939 in the following note to the Netherlands Foreign Office, the last prewar warning of which the exact text has been preserved.

NOTE

FROM: Her Netherlands Majesty's Minister in Berlin
TO: Netherlands Foreign Minister, The Hague

"It seems that two weeks ago the decision was taken to force the Polish crisis to explode not after, but before the great Nazi party convention of September. Hence all military furloughs have been cancelled as of July 20 and the first signs of German activity can probably be expected from August 15 on. For this future military activity preparations are already under way in the shape of troop concentrations towards East Prussia and also towards Silesia and Slovakia. This has given rise to stories in the English and French press about an intended occupation of Slovakia, which stories, however, are premature.

Plans now in the process of preparation at General Staff headquarters are to push forward simultaneously to the northeast and to the southeast, i.e., towards Memel and towards Slovakia as far as Ruthenia. Thus Poland would be completely surrounded, leaving only the theoretical possibility of rescue by the Russians. In that respect one is more and more inclined to doubt here whether Russia would be prepared to conclude an alliance with England. . . . If, however, such an alliance should come into being, it is assumed that Russia will first await what England would do, and it is believed that England would, in view of the situation in China, think twice before coming to the succor of Poland, which is geographically almost imposible.

Indications for the above suppositions are:

1) The press campaign against Poland, which is on the rise again after having abated for a few weeks.

2) The vicious campaign against England, which is openly being accused of desiring the destruction of Germany by Russia and Poland.

3) A remark by the British Ambassador who, some ten days ago, said to me that he did not agree with those who expected a lull until September. This view was confirmed by two other members of the British Embassy, who said they expected August to be the critical month.

4) The reply of some officials of the Ministry of Propaganda to my question as to when I should take my holidays: "We all take our leave before August 1, and you would be well advised to do the same."

Two very reliable sources informed me that the Führer has made it abundantly clear to the General Staff that he wants the Polish question settled this year. In this connection I may point out that "the Polish question" is by no means limited to Danzig, but involves the Corridor and Posen, in other words the whole question of the previous German-Polish border.

> The Minister:
> Haersma de With

When the Germans invaded Holland all official documents were burned, both at the Legation in Berlin and at the Foreign Office in The Hague. This dispatch escaped because it had been sent for comment to our Minister in London, Count van Limburg Stirum. He was a man of marked personality who, when he was Minister in Berlin, never hid his strong anti-Nazi sentiments. In one of his reports from Berlin he wrote, "Behind the shining shield of their love for peace they are whetting their sword"—a phrase which has always stayed in my mind because it applies to nearly all totalitarian regimes and because, as always, so many failed to look behind the shield.

In spite of all these indications of a crisis in August, with possible military consequences, outwardly life went on normally and peacefully. Every day was sunny. We played tennis and swam at the Blau-Weiss tennis club; we took long walks in the Grunewald; we made excursions to the Wannsee and other picturesque nearby lakes; my little daughter enjoyed her new sandbox in the garden. But behind the radiant stinging sun we saw the stormclouds building up on the horizon. The diplomatic and foreign community was pervaded by a feeling of impending doom.

Under these depressing circumstances no one felt much like taking a holiday. Still, I was entitled to a week's leave, and with the diplomat's inborn political curiosity I decided to take a personal look at the next object of Hitler's greed: Danzig and the Polish Corridor.

Just then an invitation arrived from a friend who had been appointed honorary Consul-General in Danzig, Jonkheer van der Maessen de Sombreff. He was a lover of the good things in life, a connoisseur of good food, fine wines, beautiful women, and interesting company. I accepted his invitation happily but chose to stay in a hotel in the nearby holiday resort of Zoppot, famous for its *concours hippique* and its casino. This little seaside resort had already been fashionable in the days of Imperial Germany and its location on the northwestern tip of the territory of the Free City of Danzig had led to its development into a luxurious international tourist center with plenty of gambling and entertainment. Circumstances favored its success: holidaying Poles and tourists mixed with German, Polish, and League of Nations officials trying to make the best of life in this artificial ministate created by the Treaty of Versailles.

The idea behind this creation was not so bad. Reverting to its historic status as a free Hansa city, Danzig was to constitute demilitarizd international territory, supervised on behalf of the League of Nations by a High Commissioner and providing a neutral port for both Poland and East Prussia, its traditional customers. Like many such an artificial construction, it probably *could* have worked if both parties had wanted it to. Since neither did, it failed. Poland, which wanted a port of its own, soon began to construct a large artificial harbor at Gdynia or Gdansk at the northern tip of the Corridor, which attracted much of Danzig's trade. The predominantly German population of the Free City was allowed political representation in the Senate. After the Nazi takeover in Germany, the senate was completely dominated by the Nazi Party, constantly working to reincorporate Danzig in the Reich. Thus the Free City of Danzig, intended as a zone of peaceful cooperation for the benefit of all, turned into a free fighting arena for competing and intriguing forces.

To the casual visitor, this depressing situation was not immediately visible. The days—and the nights—were full of fun and laughter. My colleague Willem Gevers, Attaché in Warsaw, had also arrived in Zoppot for a short holiday, prompted by the same instinctive curiosity that had attracted me. Thanks to the hospitality of our host and his cheerful circle of friends we never had a dull moment. In the evening we enjoyed excellent seafood from the Baltic and danced or tried our luck at the casino; during the daytime we visited the picturesque old Hansa city of Danzig and the impressive new Polish harbor of Gdynia. One day we were guests at the residence of the High Commissioner, Carl Jacob Burckhardt, a Swiss of high reputation. We were entertained by his beautiful wife, for he himself was constantly occupied with the latest crisis in the territory. This time Nazi *Gauleiter* (District Commissioner) Forster had accused the Poles of planning a nocturnal surprise takeover of the

Free City's railway network. In return the Poles accused the Germans of having secretly brought SA and SS units into the territory in violation of its demilitarized status. The Nazis denied it indignantly.

If the Polish allegations were true, they were strong evidence of Germany's aggressive plans, so I decided to check on them. The American Consul-General, Kuykendall, told me he had reported to his government that during the night he often heard military units marching past his residence. This report had apparently leaked out, as many things did in that small artificial community, and the Nazis had fiercely attacked Kuykendall.

"You know very well," the Nazi Gauleiter had barked, "that there isn't a single German solider within the territory of the Free City."

"Listen," said the American matter-of-factly. "I am not a party to your quarrel, but I can't help it that my house is situated on the main road from Danzig to Zoppot, and that I have one pair of ears and one pair of eyes, which I simply cannot shut every time your troops come marching by!"

I decided to test Kuykendall's report. That very night, after a late and festive evening, instead of returning directly to my hotel I took the road from Zoppot to Danzig. I did not have to wait long. The misty beams of my headlights soon showed a military unit approaching. I parked my car on the shoulder to let the troops pass. In the eerie silence of the night the only sound was the perfect rhythm of rows of strictly disciplined soldiers' boots on the pavement. Occasionally there would be a harsh but subdued German command. In the silence and mist I felt as though I were seeing an army of ghosts, and when the apparition had again disappeared into the fog I almost wondered if I had been hallucinating. But I knew better. These were Nazi units, whether military or paramilitary, training for the big day.

I recall a conversation with the Polish Harbor Commissioner, Moderow. To me he represented the true East European type—a hard, square Slavic skull, shaven and glistening, which seemed to me expressive of a hard, square character. His youthful, blue-eyed wife used to tease him by saying, "My husband is called Moderow, but he should be called Dodorov, because he always wants to go to sleep (in French, *faire dodo*)"—and this was obviously not to the taste of the lively Helenka.

Our conversation inevitably turned to the Danzig problem and I asked him, "Do you see any possibility of a *modus vivendi* with the Germans concerning Danzig and the Corridor?"

His features took on as hard a look as his skull when he replied "Such a possibility I would only be able to see after we had lost a war—and *that* possibility I don't see for the time being."

Another symptom of the local atmosphere was the showing of the fiercely anti-Nazi American film *Confessions of a Nazi Spy*, which had been enjoying great success in France and England in spite of strong German protests. When I saw, somewhat to my surprise, that the film was playing in Gdynia, I insisted on seeing it. The most interesting aspect was not that it was an excellent movie, but rather that such a fiercely anti-Nazi film had been produced in the neutral United States and was now being shown here, right on the German border, at the center of the next crisis. And most typical of the situation in that summer of 1939 was the fanatical acclaim of the film's Polish audience.

I reported all these impressions to our Foreign Office under the title "The Dance on the Volcano." I mentioned the signs I had witnessed of the coming test of strength: the Germans' firm determination to force a crisis, the equally strong Polish determination not to give in, the signs of stepped-up military preparations in and around the demilitarized Free City, the expectation that as soon as war broke out Danzig would declare itself part of the Reich, and the presence of German military forces in East Prussia, ready to move in.

The report was well received and brought me a compliment from the Secretary-General of our Foreign Office during my next visit to The Hague. In one of his typical down-to-earth comments he summed up the situation: "It's sad to say, but as I see it Poland is a lost cause anyhow between those two big bullies."

He was right. The Polish situation was hopeless, as it always had been when Poland's two powerful neighbors got together, as they were about to do again. Driving back to Berlin from Danzig I witnessed a sign of things to come. On the badly paved road through the Polish Corridor there approached a heavy cloud of swirling dust from which emerged a squadron of Polish lancers. It was an impressive and stylish yet almost medieval sight. The long lances, carried straight up, made a solid block, as one sees in old paintings. Magnificent horses, magnificent riders—but I shivered to think what would happen when these men with this equipment had to battle German tanks. On Hitler's birthday in April, I had seen them passing in review in Berlin, six abreast, like a wall of steel.

The atmosphere in Berlin on my return was even more oppressive and ominous, although life continued in its "normal" way.

On Saturday, August 23, the German-Netherlands Society held a dinner at the Golf Club in Wannsee, a few miles outside Berlin. It was a balmy summer evening; the setting sun cast a golden glow over the green golf links and the shimmering lake, making as idyllic and peaceful a setting as one could imagine. Staatsrat Helfrich, the President of the Society, spoke eloquently about the centuries-old friendship between Holland and Germany, a friendship that would continue no matter what. But hardly had he spoken than a wave of emotion stirred among the guests at the news which had just been broadcast and was being passed from guest to guest in excited whispers. Ribbentrop had concluded a friendship pact with Molotov! To those of us who had been concerned about the slow pace of negotiations between the Western powers and the Soviet Union over help to Czechoslovakia, this was a thunderbolt. Nazi Germany and Soviet Russia, up to then archenemies, had found each other! For weeks we had noticed that the Nazi press' usual vehement attacks on the Soviet Union had subsided, then disappeared altogether. But no one had expected this! If the first stories were accurate, Hitler now had a free hand *vis à vis* Poland and the Western powers.

The rest of August was a nightmare. Although we felt that the situation was desperate, we clung to every hint that the worst might still be avoided. Sometimes the threat that hung over Europe seemed to fade away, only to return almost immediately in a more severe form. We heard about the desperate attempts of the American and British governments to avoid the disaster. We heard about the emotional appeals made by French Ambassador Robert Coulondre and British Ambassador Neville Henderson to Hitler personally, in which, in exasperation, they "said everything that their hearts moved them to say as one human being to another." It was all in vain. Hiding his intentions behind new "peace proposals," Hitler deliberately aimed for war. He instructed his generals to prepare for his final order to open hostilities— probably in the early morning of August 26.

This did not prevent Hitler from urging Ambassador Henderson, on the afternoon of August 25, to transmit his latest "peace offer" to London as soon as possible. But hardly had Sir Neville left the room when Hitler called in General Wilhelm Keitel and confirmed his order for the attack on Poland:

"Tomorrow at dawn!"*

In spite of all the signs of impending war, many in

* Joachim C. Fest, *Hitler* (Paris: Gallimard, 1973), p. 815.

the West, perhaps even a majority, even at that last moment still thought the world would get by. A typical example of this optimism occurred in the United States Embassy in Berlin on August 28.

The situation in this Embassy was most unusual for such tense times. After the "Kristallnacht," the anti-Jewish pogrom of November 1938, the U.S. government had recalled its Ambassador from Berlin as a demonstration of disapproval. From that moment on the leadership of the Embassy was in the hands of Counselor Alexander Kirk, a skeptical, businesslike American with much charm, a great sense of humor, and very little liking for the Nazis. Next in charge was my friend Donald Heath, First Secretary, who thus had to bear an exceptionally heavy responsibility for his rank. Don had, as he told me much later, an additional secret responsibility: Secretary of the Treasury Henry J. Morgenthau had ordered him to transmit to Morgenthau any political message he might receive from the German Finance Minister, Hjalmar Schacht, or any other news that Heath considered important enough.

On August 28 Heath thought the situation sufficiently serious to warn Morgenthau about the danger of impending war. Morgenthau was then in Finland and had appointed Merle Cochran in the U.S. Embassy in Paris as his personal representative and coordinator in charge of his contacts in Europe. It had also been agreed that Heath would couch any message about the danger of war in terms of an impending baseball match. Thus, on the 28th, Heath telephoned to Cochran his message about a baseball game due to take place in a few days. Cochran was supposed to transmit the message in the same language to Morgenthau in Finland. By unfortunate coincidence, however, Cochran had that same morning, after consulting several colleagues, informed Morgenthau that the unanimous view of the U.S. Ambassadors in Europe was that they did not expect war. As a result of these contradictory messages, Morgenthau failed to understand Heath's baseball warning.*

An alternative version has it that Heath's alarming message was deliberately watered down at the U.S. Embassy in Paris in order not to contradict its own earlier optimistic dispatch.

Had Morgenthau received and understood the full impact of Heath's warning it probably would have made no difference to the course of events. The incident is proof that many well-informed diplomats, even on August 28, 1939, three days before the outbreak of war, did not really expect it.

The U.S. Chargé in Berlin was no exception in this respect. When Heath told him that he considered war very likely, Kirk laughed wholeheartedly and said, "Even someone as stupid as I can see that there will be no war!"*

* Information of Donald Heath to the author.

Two

FALL WEISS

IN THE MEANTIME in Danzig the Greek tragedy continued toward a treacherous last act involving a Trojan horse.

On August 25 a German training ship, the cruiser *Schleswig-Holstein*, arrived in Danzig for a friendship visit and moored opposite Westerplatte, the Polish military base. The commander and his officers paid the usual courtesy calls on the High Commissioner of the League of Nations and on the representative of the Polish government, Minister Chodacki. The return calls proceeded with the perfect correctness one might expect on a German man-of-war. The official visitors to the *Schleswig-Holstein* did not know that before entering the harbor the cruiser had in open sea taken on 225 heavily armed shock troops from six German minesweepers. While the Polish Minister inspected the immaculate honor guard of cadets on the main deck, these 225 men sat packed in the hold, almost choking in their confined quarters. None on board knew the real purpose of this "friendship visit" except the Commander, Captain Wilhelm Kleikamp, for only he knew of the secret instruction "GK dos. 250/39."* Its contents weighed so heavily on his conscience that during a reception given by High Commissioner Burckhardt, he could keep silent no longer and said to his Swiss host in a subdued voice, "I have a terrible instruction, which my conscience cannot justify."† But he executed it precisely when on August 26 he received the code word "Fall Weiss" ("Case White"). At 17:00 hours he welcomed on board Senate President Arthur Greiser and Police Commander General Eberhardt. With these two reliable Nazis he made the last-minute arrangements, which he inscribed in his ship's log: "The company of SS troops receives the order to stand by at 21:30 for disembarkation. From 19:00 hours on, the quayside will be evacuated by reliable policemen over a distance of 300 meters on both sides. The big lights on the quayside will be extinguished. . . ." But when everything was ready for disembarkation, a counterorder suddenly arrived: Stop everything! Attack temporarily postponed.

The reason for the cancellation was to become clear only later. On August 26 England had concluded a formal alliance with Poland and Mussolini had informed Hitler that he was not ready for war. Furious about this British and Italian perfidy, Hitler decided to postpone the attack in the hope of keeping England out by new assurances and proposals for peace. But on August 30, fed

*"*Das Erste Todeskommando des Zweiten Weltkrieges,*" *Quick,* Sept. 1974, pp. 66 ff.
†Carl Jacob Burckhardt, *Meine Danziger Mission, 1937–1939* (Zurich: Fretz und Wasmuth, 1960), p. 351.

up with waiting, Hitler served an ultimatum on Poland to send a negotiator immediately to Berlin "with full powers," that is: to accept Hitler's demands. In reply Poland ordered general mobilization.

That evening of August 30, 1939, the High Commissioner of the League of Nations for the Free City of Danzig gave an official dinner in honor of the German warship which, he suspected, had come to end the city's free status. It was an historic meal, drenched with forebodings of disaster. "The most terrible and gloomy dinner I have ever attended," Madame Burckhardt told me later, when she described the evening to me.

At that moment when the eyes of the world were fixed fearfully on the Free City of Danzig, all its leading authorities were gathered at the dinner: the President of the Danzig Senate, Greiser, the Nazi Gauleiter Albert Forster, the Polish Minister Chodacki, and the German Commander of the *Schleswig-Holstein*. They all knew that war might erupt at any moment. The two Nazi leaders knew of Hitler's ultimatum to Poland; the German naval officer knew what awful task he was to perform; the Polish Minister knew that his country had ordered mobilization; the High Commissioner knew that on August 11 Hitler had said to him, "At the smallest incident I shall destroy the Poles without warning so that afterwards not a trace of Poland can be found. . . . I shall attack like lightening with the full power of a mechanized army."*

* Joachim C. Fest, *Hitler* (Paris: Gallimard, 1973), p. 804.

But none of them dared reveal his knowledge or speak of things to come. The diplomatic performance was enacted to the bitter end.

Silence reigned around the dinner table; even the beautiful dish of *queues d'écrevisses* could not break the ice. As the crawfish, a special delicacy from the Vistula, lay on the individual plates with the Danzig crest, everyone waited awkwardly for the host to propose a toast of welcome. But High Commissioner Burckhardt could not make himself utter false words of welcome to the "friendly visitors" whose hostile purpose he could imagine only too well. Finally, as a compromise between his conscience and the requirement of protocol, he silently raised his glass to each of the guests individually.

Everyone was on edge. Talk was dull and strained, limited to casual remarks about the persisting warm weather, the lack of rain, and the imminent opening of the hunting season. Even the last subject seemed to take on a double meaning under the circumstances. Immediately after coffee the German guests rose in unison and, clicking their heels in Prussian fashion, took their leave.

The next day the High Commissioner and his wife received as a token of gratitude a large picture of the German warship framed in black with a black ribbon bearing the name *"Schleswig-Holstein"* in gold letters. This souvenir, meant as a gesture of politeness gave more the impression of a funeral announcement for the League of Nations' role in Danzig.

And so it proved to be.

On that same August 31, at 18:35, the *Schleswig-*

Holstein again received the code word "Fall Weiss." The moment of attack had been fixed one hour earlier than previously. For the rest the whole ritual was repeated, except that now the SS troops got their precise orders: tomorrow at dawn, with massive artillery support from the cruiser, they would attack the Polish strongpoint, Westerplatte. In his briefing the Nazi General omitted to mention that the Poles had installed an elaborate system of underground bunkers and artillery that had turned this innocent-looking island into an almost impenetrable fortress, which could at best be conquered by dive bombers. The SS troops had no maps or aerial photographs and their cases of grenades, when opened, contained only practice munitions. But they were confident; they would be covered by the enormous firing power of the 13,000-ton cruiser.

Late that evening two Gestapo men knocked loudly on the High Commissioner's front door. Burckhardt was told in no uncertain terms that he was under house arrest, that his telephone had been cut off, and that he must remain ready to receive the Nazi Gauleiter with an important message during the night.

Burckhardt answered coldly that he did not intend to wait the whole night for the Gauleiter; he would go to bed now. He needed little effort to imagine what message the Gauleiter would bring: that Danzig was being incorporated into the Reich and that the High Commissioner, last representative of the despised system of Versailles, had been relieved of his duties.

Burckhardt had a short wait. Even before first light

he was awakened. The butler, whom the Burckhardts knew was a Nazi informer and who had obsequiously served the "Excellencies" at dinner the night before, banged on the bedroom door, shouting, "Get up! This is the end of the glory! Burckhardt must come down to the Gauleiter!"

Burckhardt answered quietly that the Gauleiter would have to wait until he had dressed. When he came downstairs, the Gauleiter was nowhere to be seen yet. But the Nazi war machine had been working from the first moment with unfaltering and awesome precision. Soon he received a far more eloquent message.

While the black night sky slowly faded over East Prussia, Commander Kleikamp stood on the bridge of the *Schleswig-Holstein* tensely awaiting the moment: tomorrow at dawn, at 04:45. His eyes sharply fixed on the slow hand of his watch, he saw it reach the forty-fifth minute. At his command, "Fire!" all hell broke loose. The thunder of the ship's guns rolled over sleeping Danzig, and a sea of fire and steel poured on the Westerplatte. The Second World War had begun.

At exactly 08:00 Gauleiter Forster appeared at the High Commissioner's residence with much banging of car doors and shouting of orders, surrounded by a retinue of black uniforms and jackboots. He announced loudly to the High Commissioner: "You were the representative of the scandalous Diktat of Versailles, which has now been torn to shreds by the Fuehrer. You will have to leave the territory of Danzig within two hours. Then the swastika will be raised over the residence of the previous High Commissioner."*

The High Commissioner was prepared for this moment. With supreme disdain he turned his back on the Gauleiter and approached his waiting automobile. At that moment a new salvo exploded and several window panes of the High Commissioner's old Danziger house crashed to the floor, smashed by Nazi violence like the world of Versailles.

The attack on the Westerplatte had to be abandoned around ten in the morning because the SS troops had been decimated by heavy Polish artillery fire for which they were not prepared. By then 98 of the 225 men surviewed. †

The occupation of Danzig during the very first hours of the war, though politically spectacular and important, was only a small sideshow from the military point of view. The real attack took place farther south across the Polish border. For this, again, a deceptive scenario had been meticulously worked out to deceive the world about the responsibility for the outbreak of hostilities.

For six days a group of SS men had been waiting on the Polish border to fake a Polish attack on the German radio station at Gleiwitz on the eve of the main offensive.

* Burckhardt, *Danziger Mission,* p. 353.
†*Das Erste Todeskommando des Zweiten Weltkrieges,"* *Quick,* Sept. 1974, p. 71.

Dressed in Polish uniforms, the SS men captured the radio station by surprise, broadcast a brief anti-German speech, and left a few drugged concentration camp inmates, significantly code-named "canned goods," dying on the spot as casualties to prove there had been a Polish attack. This "infamous Polish aggression" could not, of course, pass without retaliation, as Hitler explained in the Reichstag the next day. At daybreak, just as the guns of the *Schleswig-Holstein* were thundering destruction over the Westerplatte in Danzig, Hitler's armored columns roared across the Polish border and German airplanes swooped down on the Polish airfields, destroying most of Poland's 405 planes on the ground.

From then on the German ground forces, covered by the Luftwaffe, were safe from air attack and moved forward irresistibly. Some 1000 German tanks, divided into a Northern and a Southern Army Group, rumbled across the Polish plains, seizing the bulk of the Polish army in an iron pincer movement. The Polish campaign made a horrifying display of the power and efficiency of the armed force Hitler had created from nothing.

Before the outbreak of war several Military Attachés in Berlin had expressed the view that the German and Polish forces would probably keep each other in balance. This, they reported to their governments, could lead to a stalemate that might open the door to a possible compromise peace in which Hitler would, of course, obtain his wishes regarding Danzig and the Corridor, but which need not cost the West anything. Some serious observers in Berlin even continued to repeat the fairy tale that many of the German tanks which had so gloriously occupied Vienna and Prague were made of cardboard.

Pretty tough cardboard, as the Polish lancers found when they fell under deadly fire charging the German armor with their lances. Yet even then in Berlin some Western diplomats shook their heads in pity and said to one another, "This just goes to show that when it comes to the test of military power you cannot really rely on a country like Poland."

But eight months later their own forces would do no better.

For weeks the *Reichssender Berlin* fed us day-to-day and hour-to-hour victory communiqués, preceded by martial fanfares. During those few weeks, when the world barely realized what was happening, the war in Poland was decided. A bragging and boisterous victory speech by Hitler—and then silence descended on destroyed Poland and the smoldering ruins of Warsaw. Independent Poland had been obliterated from the map, just as Hitler had predicted. He left the rest of his prediction, "so that no trace of it can be found afterwards," to the Nazi party organizations moving in behind the army. Conquered Poland was organized into a *General-Gouvernement Polen*, a high-sounding title for a colony to be exploited to the bitter end.

In the Dutch Legation in Berlin, I got the task of handling all questions about occupied Poland. This was a useless and purely theoretical responsibility, as I saw at once, when my application to visit the *General-Gou-*

vernement Polen was abruptly refused. Colleagues from other Missions fared no better; an impenetrable Nazi curtain had descended around Poland. What happened behind that curtain was only whispered in Berlin—how after the military victory the Nazi Party took over from the Wehrmacht, how military officers protested the bestial cruelty with which the party carried out its "historic mission," a mission clearly formulated by Gouvernor-General Hans Frank: to exterminate the Polish intelligentsia and to turn the rest of the Polish nation into slaves for the master race of the Third Reich.

Then our turn came.

Three

ENTER THE GHOST INFORMER

OUR FIRST WARNING reached us on October 9. By a macabre quirk of fate I had a chance to recall the whole sequence of events exactly seven months later. They say that a dying person, during his last moments, may see the events of his life again in flashback. Something similar happened to me that terrible May evening in Berlin, when our country's death sentence had finally been passed.

That was on May 9, 1940. I was trying to find my way through pitch-dark blacked-out Berlin by the poor light shining from my car's slit eyes. The strict blackout regulations required that headlights be painted black except for a slit one centimeter high by five centimeters wide, with the beam directed downward. The narrow rays groped their way along the edge of sidewalks and between the fleeing legs of pedestrians. My irritatingly slow pace was extremely frustrating because every minute counted. I had been summoned from a dinner party given by Donald Heath, the U.S. Chargé d'affaires, to come to the Netherlands Chancery immediately. Such an urgent message could only mean one thing: the attack on our country, on the Western front, on the world's peace, so long feared, was coming now.

Seven months had passed since that first warning on October 9. Seven months of murderous nervous tension, occasionally mounting to a climax, then receding. It was like a nightmare of standing rooted to one spot on a beach, watching each wave come closer and closer to our feet, wondering whether the next one would engulf us. We could not flee. So far, the surf had always receded at the last minute. But each time it returned, it came closer to our feet. This time would it swell into a spring tide, swamping all Europe, chasing streams of armies and refugees ahead of it, finally swallowing them all?

Those seven months had taught us that we could never be certain until the very last moment. But every time the probability of war increased; every time we had less chance of waking from our bad dream.

On my right a slit of light approached. In the impenetrable darkness I could not judge the distance, but suddenly the approaching light halted abruptly, with an angry jangling and the groan of brakes. Although I could not see exactly what had happened I realized that I had barely escaped being run over by a Berlin streetcar. Would the Nazi war machine, like the streetcar, stop at our border at the last minute? Everything in those days came back to that one dominant question.

If the streetcar ran here, this must be the Kurfuer-stendamm. Now I had to turn left, toward the Gedaecht-

niskirche, then on the Budapesterstrasse, across the
bridge and left to our Chancery in the Rauchstrasse.
That route I knew by heart; as I drove, my mind wandered back through the past.

In October 1939 our legation had its first contact with
a mysterious figure who was to dominate our lives like a
hovering ghost during the subsequent months. He was
the "connection" of our Military Attaché, Major G. J.
Sas. No one but Sas knew this man; no one had ever seen
him; no one knew his name or his exact position; some
even doubted his existence. But from October 1939 on
he made his presence felt more and more frequently
with ominous warnings which often seemed correct at
first, but as often did not materialize. Sas succeeded in
guarding his informer's identity until after the war. Even
the Third Reich's effective secret police did not discover
who he was until early 1945, a surprising circumstance
because Sas was really not very careful about the information he received. Every new communication so ob-
sessed him that he had to inform, in confidence, all the
diplomatic members of the Legation. I have never understood why the Reich's omnipresent intelligence services did not discover these contacts much earlier. This
very fact made some of us suspect the informer's reliability. It was hard to believe that anyone could feed such
valuable secret information so regularly to a foreign mission without being detected—unless the informant acted
with the secret approval or even upon instruction of his
superiors.
   Major Sas had met his contact while he was stationed

in Berlin as Military Attaché in 1936–37; when he and this German colleague had become close personal friends. In 1938 Sas had left Berlin to become Head of Military Operations at the General Staff in The Hague. In April 1939, however, the increasing danger of war made it advisable to send Sas, with his valuable Berlin experience, back there. On his arrival, Sas immediately resumed his friendship with his fiercely anti-Nazi colleague, from whom he soon started to receive much useful secret information. At that early stage his informer even hinted at a conspiracy to oust Hitler. Those who had not lived in Nazi Germany might find it hard to believe that even high officers would be prepared to take action that would normally be considered treacherous; but we who knew how the regime was hated in certain circles could understand.

It would be wrong to assume that Sas or our Legation was guided exclusively by the intelligence received from Sas' "connection." Such information was, of course, always evaluated in the context of the situation and checked against information received from other sources. But it was our main guideline, and Sas never doubted the reliability of the informer's news, even when events sometimes contradicted it later on. Sas alone knew how well placed the informer was to obtain the most secret and authentic information. When we wondered why the informer's activity was not discovered, Sas would smile knowingly and say, "My connection is so highly placed that he is above all suspicion."

And so, during the fall and winter, the ghost of Sas'

secret informer haunted the gloomy old Chancery at Rauchstrasse 10, sometimes forgotten, sometimes disowned, sometimes clearly belied by the facts, sometimes derided, sometimes denied in his very existence—until suddenly he would grip us with a new warning.

He began to warn us specifically about the danger for Holland after the Nazi victory over Poland. Sas himself, in late September 1939, reported that once the Polish campaign was successfully concluded an attack against the West seemed inevitable. And this time, he said, the Germans would not repeat their military mistake of 1914, when they respected Dutch neutrality by marching around the province of Limburg, the protruding southern "leg" on which the Netherlands stands on the map.

"This time," Sas wrote on September 28 to the Dutch Commander-in-Chief, General Reynders, "they will carry out the alternative originally conceived by General von Schlieffen in 1911 and thrust with a strong right wing directly through the southern leg." This was the so-called Schlieffen plan, which was abandoned at the last minute in 1914 in order to respect Dutch neutrality.

In the same report Sas also predicted that the tension in the West would make itself felt in about six weeks, in the first half of November. Both predictions were to become bitter reality; but at that moment Sas' superiors in Holland hardly took them seriously.

During October, some 65 to 70 German divisions were transferred from Poland to Western Germany, where they were placed not far from the Dutch and Belgian borders. To reassure us, Quartermaster-General Werner von Tippelskirch assured Sas on October 7 that these were "purely defensive dispositions." The Secretary-General of the German Foreign Office, the Auswaertige Amt, explained the move to the Belgian Ambassador and the Dutch Minister with the remark, "After all, we've got to put these troops up *somewhere* now that they've finished in Poland!"

Sas was not fooled. Two days later he told his informer, "You bet, soon things will start popping in the West, and this time we, the Dutch, will not escape the danger. A frontal attack on the West through the Netherlands is inevitable. The Germans will not repeat the mistake they made in 1914 by marching around the province of Limburg. This time they'll take the shortest route and march right through."

The informer replied that no such decision had been made, but he promised to investigate. A few days later he assured Sas, "A plan for a thrust through Belgium is at present being studied in the office of Chief-of-Staff Halder. *This plan avoids violating Netherlands territory.*"*

Sas always made it a point to pass on the information from his informer immediately to the Belgian Military Attaché, Colonel Goethals. Thus his warnings usually reached the Belgian government soon after the Dutch government in an almost identical form, but usually mit-

---

* Testimony of (then) Major General G. J. Sas in *Report of the Netherlands Parliamentary Commission of Inquiry* vol. Ic, pp. 208–209; Jean van Welkenhuyzen, "Les Advertissements qui venaient de Berlin," p. 3.

igated by Goethals' personal comments. One must take into account Goethals' personality and views. This excellent Belgian officer was a rare combination of a brilliant fighter and an intellectual, a career officer and a doctor of political science, a mathematician and a humanist. His pupils at the Artillery School were taught above all to be *gentlemen,* which in his words meant to apply moderation and dignity in everything. This view induced him to treat Sas' warnings with detached balance. He reported them faithfully, but diminished their impact by pointing out their doubtful reliability and by mentioning alternate possibilities. In this attitude he found a kindred soul in his ambassador, Vicomte Jacques Davignon, father of the later Commissioner of the European Community. Ambassador Davignon's policy was to report all information to his government, but to prevent Belgium from making any move in panic which could compromise its strict neutrality and serve as an excuse for a German attack.

What happened to that first main warning on October 9 was typical of the treatment of all future warnings by the Belgian Embassy. Since this particular warning was, of course, of vital importance to Belgium, Sas rushed to the Belgian Embassy. Goethals had not yet returned from lunch, so Sas waited in front of the Embassy to be sure to catch him. Before long Ambassador Davignon himself arrived and kindly invited him in. Sas told the Ambassador that he had heard from a reliable source that the German General Staff was studying plans for a push through Belgium but avoiding Dutch territory.

The Ambassador meticulously took down the information, then questioned Sas on the identity and reliability of his source. On the first point Sas regretted that he could not reveal his source's identity; on the second he said he felt absolutely sure of the man's reliability. Finally Sas expressed his deep sympathy with Belgium, which, he emphasized, was in great danger, and left.*

Immediately upon Goethals' return the Ambassador consulted with him about the alarming news. As usual they were of one mind: report the information to the Belgian authorities as it was received, but at the same time see to it that these did not get so alarmed as to take precipitate action. Consequently Goethals sent the following cypher to the Belgian General Staff:

The Dutch Military Attaché has heard from a German friend whom he considers reliable and well placed: A German march through Belgium is at this moment being studied at the bureau of Chief-of-Staff General Halder; this plan avoids passing through the Netherlands.

Goethals then added his own comment:

Although this information must of course receive full attention, there is reason to believe that such a study had already been worked out, amongst other ones, and that the present circumstances have led to an up-dating or an addition. This does not mean that its execution has been decided.

And finally he pointed to the reassuring explanation which General von Tippelskirch had given two days ago to Sas.

The next day, October 10, Ambassador Davignon

* Davignon, "*Berlin 1936–1940*", Ed. Univ., Paris-Bruxelles, 1951, p. 21.

further weakened the effect of the warning in a very long telegram in which he cast some doubt on Sas' secret informer.

The Dutch Military Attaché is of the opinion that his informer is reliable. He also considers him well placed to obtain information in the sense that he works in the War Ministry but in an office which has nothing to do with the General Staff. In addition he is not a person of top rank: far from that. One can even wonder whether he has not been instructed to transmit to us the information in question. For the discipline here is such that one may well wonder whether revelations are at all possible. They could be meant either to fool the Dutch or to induce us to commit a "faux pas" which could give Germany a pretext to intervene.

The Ambassador then went on to argue that the decision would ultimately depend on political considerations, and those favored keeping Belgium neutral.

Before sending off this cypher Davignon consulted his Netherlands colleague on the value to be attributed to Sas' message. As a result he added the following postscript:

Jonkheer van Haersma de With does not exaggerate its importance. He feels it is only the resumption of a study, i.e. one possibility under consideration, not a decision taken. The Dutch Minister does not know the name of the informer of his Military Attaché. His name must remain secret in order not to lose a source of information. The man is not being rewarded. He is a fierce enemy of the present German regime, which moves him to make revelations.*

---

* The full text of Davignon's telegram is reproduced by Jean van Welkenhuyzen in "Les Avertissements qui venaient de Berlin," pp. 12–16.

Thus the alarming news with which Sas had rushed to the Belgian Embassy was in the end presented to Brussels rather reassuringly as contingency planning. This is certainly not what the informer had meant. He had been reassuring only on one point: that Holland would be spared.

On that one reassuring point he was wrong.

Four

THE NOVEMBER ALARM

THE INFORMATION from Sas' connection seemed more reassuring to Holland than the facts warranted. As would often occur in the subsequent months, the informer was well briefed, but his news was not always correct in detail and was sometimes outdated by the time we had transmitted it. We now know that as early as September 27 Hitler announced to his military leaders his firm intention to launch an offensive in the West before the end of 1939. We also know that on October 9 Hitler, in his "Directive No. 6 for the Conduct of the War," ordered all preparations for "Fall Gelb" (Case Yellow), the offensive in the West, and that on October 19 and 29 he issued further "marching directives" for that offensive. However, all these instructions, contrary to the informer's first warnings, *did* include an offensive through the southern provinces of the Netherlands, or at least through the protruding province of Limburg.

Sas' informer apparently learned this too. At their next secret meeting, on October 22 or 23, he appeared deeply depressed and admitted to Sas, "My friend, you were right; now it is also the turn of the Netherlands."

The Fuehrer, he explained, was considering an offensive through both Belgium and the Netherlands. If he decided on it, the date would be set later, depending on the weather, but probably not before the second half of November.*

Sas immediately cabled this message to his Commander-in-Chief, General Reynders. From then on, as he testified after the war before the Dutch Parliamentary Commission that investigated Holland's role in World War II, his good relations with the Commander-in-Chief changed overnight. Bad news was unwelcome, and its bearer always suffers.†

This was the beginning of an estrangement between these two crucially placed officers which developed into a bitter personal enmity over the reliability of Sas' secret "connection" and his warnings. The distrust was increased because only Sas knew who his ghost informer was. Once, hoping to prove his reliability, Sas revealed that the man held a high position in the German Supreme Command—an imprudent move, but one that might have been justified if it had convinced the Dutch Commander. It had the opposite effect. General Reynders and most of his colleagues would not believe that a Prussian officer would deliberately betray military secrets to an officer of the potential enemy.

The truth, even more incredible to outsiders, was that the same officer was conspiring at that moment to

* van Welkenhuyzen, "Les Avertissements," p. 33.
† *Netherlands Parliamentary Commission of Inquiry*, Vol. Ic, p. 209.

revive earlier plans to liquidate Hitler. For weeks General Franz Halder, the Army Chief-of-Staff, carried a loaded revolver in his pocket whenever he visited the Reichskanzlei, planning to use it on Hitler. After October 14 Halder went even further and ordered Colonel Helmuth Groscurth, Liaison Officer of Counterintelligence at headquarters in Zossen, to draw up a plan for a *coup d'état* with his secret resistance group. At the same time Sas's informer drafted a so-called "study" that included a plan of action, a list of leading Nazis to be eliminated, and a list of candidates for a provisional government under General Ludwig Beck, previous Chief-of-Staff. This list would later determine the fate of a great many resistance leaders.* At about the same time, Sas' connection helped draft an appeal to the German nation accusing Hitler of having ordered an offensive in the West in violation of Holland's and Belgium's neutrality, a crime bound to cause untold misery to Germany.

Two of the informer's co-conspirators presented this theme even more emphatically and convincingly in a memorandum entitled "The Threatening Disaster," which said plainly that the execution of Hitler's plan for an offensive in the West would spell the end of Germany as it then existed. The decision for an offensive through neutral Holland and Belgium thus meant a decision about the future of Germany. The pamphlet concluded that the offensive had to be prevented, and the only way to do so was to overthrow Hitler. Rarely has a prophecy

---

* Peter Hoffmann, *Widerstand, Staatsstreich, Attentat* (Munich: Piper), pp. 167, 716.

shown such correct foresight! The unusual frankness and conviction of this document are not diminished because the authors never carried out their coup.

From October 22 on, the Chief-of-Staff, General Halder, knew that Hitler intended to order the offensive in the West for Sunday, November 12, to be confirmed a week in advance. For days he and Commander-in-Chief General Walther von Brauchitsch did their utmost to dissuade Hitler. They only aroused his irritation, then his fury. The conflict culminated in a stormy conversation on November 5, but the generals failed to draw the consequence—and their revolvers.

All this was, of course, known only to the conspirators. Obviously we too knew nothing of the resistance plan in the Ober Kommando der Wehrmacht, although the informer had vaguely mentioned the possibility to Sas. We were more disturbed by developments from The Hague. One bad day our Legation had a visit from a retired Dutch staff officer who had been Military Attaché in Berlin during World War I, and who came to see some old friends. Soon, however, the grapevine from The Hague informed us that his real task was to find out how seriously Sas' warnings should be taken. Our visitor was a charming gentleman, a typical officer of the old school, who had made his career before the rise of the Nazi regime and who consequently had no inkling of its ruthlessness. His innocence became evident when he told us how he got his information. The best system, he said, was simply to be frank. So he asked his old German buddies, "Listen, we hear a lot of stories that you people are going to attack us. Just between us: Is that true?"

He had put that question to a few retired German officers, friends from the old days. They all assured him that they had never heard of such a plan (which may even have been true because they had been retired for quite a while).

"And if there were any such plans," said the Dutch Colonel Blimp, "they would certainly have told me so, for they are good friends."

We smiled at the naive trustfulness of the old Colonel—until we learned that, on this basis, he reported to the Head of GS III (Military Intelligence) in The Hague that Major Sas' information should not be taken seriously because the man was highly strung and near a nervous breakdown.

Sas was the last man to take such criticism quietly. Breathing fire, he took the next train to The Hague (all air connections with Holland had stopped at the outbreak of war) and asked whether his reports were really believed; if not, was there any sense in continuing them? The Head of Military Intelligence assured him that his reports *were* being believed. But one of the aides to the Minister of Defense proved the contrary by showing him the Bulletin of the Intelligence Section, in which Sas' information was commented on and ridiculed.

"If my information is being handled this way, I'd better quit," Sas concluded. He took the night train back to Berlin on November 6.*

---

* At first he was reluctant to talk about what had happened to him in The Hague. He tried to bottle it up but he could not; it came out in brief outbursts and cynical sneers. After the war he told the entire story more coherently to the Parliamentary Commission of Inquiry; it appears in vol. Ic, p. 209 of the commission's report.

When he got to his hotel on the morning of the 7th, he found an urgent message from his informer asking him to visit him at home as soon as possible. This was indeed disturbing; in principle they never met at their homes. Sas took a taxi, got out a few streets from his friend's home, and walked the last blocks. A military car was parked in front of the house. This also seemed strange, but Sas went in and found his friend in full uniform, ready to leave.

"Thank goodness you are here! There is not a moment to lose! The Fuehrer has decided to launch the offensive on November 12 and it will include the invasion of your country. I advise you to return to Holland immediately and warn your government to take all necessary precautions against an attack. I myself am off to the West front now in order to try to convince Witzleben and his consorts to prevent an offensive. But I don't think I stand much of a chance. For heaven's sake, see to it that all defensive precautions are taken in Holland—above all that the Meuse bridges are blown up!"

Sas did not hesitate to follow his friend's advice. He informed The Hague that he would be returning immediately with important new information and took the night train to The Hague—for the second time in a week.

On his arrival he was taken straight into a small meeting of Cabinet Ministers, consisting of the Prime Minister, the Ministers of Foreign Affairs and of Defense, and Commander-in-Chief Reynders. Sas very emotionally—as he himself was to admit later—reported his informer's news. He could not know (nor was he told) that the same news had been received several days earlier from the British Minister in The Hague, Sir Neville Bland. This earlier information explained why the Ministers proved far less surprised or impressed than Sas had expected. Except for the Minister of Defense, they were skeptical and even sarcastic, and the Prime Minister openly said that they had no faith in his reports. This only increased Sas' exasperation. At one point he jumped up, raised two fingers as in an oath, and said he could swear that the attack would take place on the 12th. To this the Prime Minister replied icily that one could not swear to something that had not yet occurred.*

Sas' distress increased the next day, Thursday, November 9, when a visit to the Department of Defense convinced him that no real defensive measures were being taken. He faced a crisis of conscience. We were within a few days of an attack of unparalleled magnitude on our country. He, the Military Attaché in Berlin, responsible for military information, knew an attack would take place on Sunday, knew the plan of action—and the government simply did not believe him, or at least they did not *do* anything.

All this was enough to drive Sas almost crazy. Desperately he tried every means to assure that precautions would be taken against the attack. First he visited the Commander-in-Chief of the Navy, without success. Then he went to see the former Prime Minister, Hendrik Colijn, in those days the grand old man of Dutch politics and to many the epitome of patriotism and relia-

* Dr. L. de Jong, *Het Koninkrijk der Nederlanden in de Tweede Wereldoorlog,* vol. 2 (The Hague: Staatsuitgeverij, 1969), p. 113.

bility. He told Colijn of the news he had received in Berlin, of his cold reception by the Cabinet Ministers, and of the disbelief at the General Staff. With great emotion he adjured him to see that something was done to put the country in a state of defense. But again Sas' excitement worked against him. That same afternoon Colijn telephoned Commander-in-Chief Reynders to say that Sas' stories should not be believed because the man was practically hysterical.

Sas then went to see a general who had previously headed the Military Intelligence. Again he received only harsh words.

As a last resort, Sas decided to appeal directly to the Queen. Quite by chance, in the center of The Hague he ran into an old friend who was Aide-de-Camp to Queen Wilhelmina, and together they hurried to the nearby Royal Palace. However, General Reynders had suspected such a move, and while Sas was nervously waiting in an anteroom he received a telephone message from General Reynders *forbidding* him to speak to the Queen. This was the last straw. The Queen, who had often expressed privately her concern about our inadequate military defenses against an attack by Hitler, would have believed him; *she* would have seen the danger. Sas was crushed, but orders were orders, his only recourse was to tell his story to the aide and urge him to inform Her Majesty. One can well imagine the effect of this last disappointment on an emotional man like Sas.

It seems unlikely that much would have changed if Sas had been able to speak to the Queen personally.

Queen Wilhelmina undoubtedly understood the danger. She had a powerful personality and had from the beginning been concerned about the rise of national socialism in Holland's strongest neighbor. She had long foreseen a possible German attack and had often expressed her concern in private.*

Even so, as a strictly constitutional monarch she could not have *ordered* military measures beyond those the Commander-in-Chief wished to take. At most, if Sas' message had reached her, she might have used her great personal influence and prestige to persuade the military leadership to order more defensive preparations.

For us in Berlin, that second week of November 1939 provided a disturbing new sensation every day.

Even as Major Sas was approaching the Netherlands Government, Dutch Minister of Foreign Affairs Eelco van Kleffens had launched a diplomatic initiative aimed at strengthening our political position by a joint Netherlands-Belgian appeal for peace. On Monday, November 6, five days before the expected attack, Queen Wilhelmina of the Netherlands and King Leopold III of Belgium together made an urgent appeal to France, Germany, and England to end the war. They surely had little hope that the appeal would stop the belligerents, but they thought it would at least discourage any one of them from attacking two neutral countries which had just called for peace.

In the country for which the appeal was meant, it had

* See the section on Queen Wilhelmina in de Jong, "Het Koninkrijk," vol. 9, The Hague 1979.

the least success: following a guideline from the Nazi government, the German newspapers published it only on the second page "without any emphasis or headlines and without comment." The guideline also informed the German press "that there was no possibility of peace." And Hitler commented to his entourage, "Those two countries [Holland and Belgium] will have to be cut down to size."

Twelve minutes that could have saved the world

The next day, Wednesday, November 8, Hitler followed a yearly tradition by delivering a rousing speech in the Buergerbraukeller in Munich to commemorate his attempted coup of 1923. Contrary to his habit, he left the crowded beer cellar as soon as he had finished speaking. Twelve minutes later a bomb exploded in the very place where Hitler had just been haranguing his followers. Seven died and sixty-three were wounded—but Hitler was still alive.

Berlin immediately buzzed with suppositions, explanations, and rumors. Goebbels' propaganda machine was first with an explanation: the bomb had been planted by the British Secret Service. Among the masses this caused a tremendous wave of sympathy for Hitler. But those less gullible looked for different explanations, and soon the wildest stories were being fed into the Berlin gossip machine: the bomb was a military attempt to get rid of Hitler; it could only have been placed by his closest collaborators; it was a Nazi propaganda trick to increase his popularity—what a clever idea!

Those of us in the Legation who knew about the impending offensive in the West were driven to despair by the failure of the bomb attack. To think that a difference of twelve minutes could have prevented the attack on Holland, saved all Western Europe from war, rid the world of this driving maniac, and perhaps opened the prospect of a negotiated peace! I remember running through the house in a fury, shouting, "Twelve minutes! Twelve minutes could have saved us!"

The Venlo incident

On the next day, Thursday, November 9, came another shock. On the German-Dutch border near the city of Venlo two British Secret Service agents were suddenly overpowered and kidnapped by Gestapo men who had lured them there by posing as representatives of a German opposition group. A Dutch lieutenant, Klop, a former assistant of Sas, who was accompanying the British, tried to resist and was shot down. The British intelligence officers were dragged over the border and abducted in a German car.

New enigmas, new questions! We cabled our Foreign Office for information immediately. The answer came back at once. Two British representatives, Captain Payne Best and Major R. H. Stevens, had been invited for a border rendezvous to discuss peace overtures with representatives of dissident German groups. This, the Foreign Office telegram explained, was not a Dutch responsibility. It was, however, a Dutch responsibility to see to it that nothing should happen contrary to Netherlands' neutrality; therefore Dutch Lieutenant Klop had been ordered to accompany the British. He had rightly defended himself and we were instructed to demand his extradition, dead or alive.

This was the none too convincing explanation with which our Minister was supposed to explain to the Auswaertige Amt the presence of a Dutch staff officer at the border meeting. The telegram unfortunately failed to mention that Best was on the official staff of the British Legation in The Hague. That information, which we learned later by chance, would at least have given us a plausible reason for sending a Dutch officer along with him.

In context, these events became even more alarming: on Wednesday a bomb attack on Hitler, immediately ascribed to the British Secret Service; on Thursday two British Secret Service agents kidnapped on the German-Dutch border, a Dutch officer in their company shot or killed; and the great offensive in the West scheduled for Sunday morning.

Our Minister in Berlin, Jonkheer van Haersma de With, a careful but shrewd old-school diplomat, realized immediately that speed was essential. Obviously the first two incidents could easily be linked and presented by German propaganda as the Dutch and the British Secret Service conniving to overthrow Hitler. An excellent excuse for the attack on Sunday!

The Minister carried out his most unpleasant and delicate démarche on the evening of Friday, November 10, the day after the Venlo incident, in a visit to Prince

Otto von Bismarck, Head of the Political Section of the Auswaertige Amt and grandson of the "Iron Chancellor." After outlining the course of events, as he knew them at that moment, the Minister explained that the Netherlands government had allowed the British representatives to visit the border because we wanted to support every attempt at restoring peace. He added soothingly that in these excited times such an incident should not be exaggerated. Juridically, the fate of the two British agents was not primarily a Dutch responsibility, but what happened to the Dutch officer was. This officer, dead or alive, must be extradited to us along with his driver. Bismarck declared that he knew nothing about the matter and ended the conversation.*

In the months that followed our Legation demanded Klop's extradition no less than nine times. On January 25, 1940, we even proposed submitting the whole question to the German-Netherlands Court of Arbitration or to the International Court of Justice. We never received a reply. As it turned out, Lieutenant Klop had been killed on the spot; Major Stevens and Captain Best survived miraculously for five and a half years in German concentration camps. †

To our surprise and initial relief the Germans published nothing about the Venlo incident for almost two weeks. Only on November 21 did the German press reveal that Stevens and Best, "the leader of the British

---

Akten zur deutschen Auswaertigen Politik, 1918–1945 Series D, vol. VIII, First Part, pp. 310–311.
† Payne Best, *The Venlo Incident* (London: Hutchinson, 1950).

intelligence service for Europe," had tried to precipitate a revolution in Germany.

We soon understood that the German reticence was not meant to play down the incident but rather to use it for maximum effect later on. It would be invaluable evidence that the Netherlands Military Intelligence Bureau (GS III) had exchanged information with and rendered services to the British Secret Service, even helping British intelligence arrange a meeting on the Dutch border between British agents and supposed German conspirators against Hitler. It provided Hitler with proof that the Dutch did not adhere to their neutrality! Fully realizing its value, Hitler had himself briefed daily about the interrogation of the British agents. On November 23 he told a meeting of military leaders what he planned to do with the information: "Belgium and Holland sympathize with France and England. The Venlo incident proves it; the man who was killed was not an Englishman but an officer of the Dutch General Staff. This was not mentioned in the press. Now the Dutch Government has asked for extradition of his body. That was one of its greatest stupidities. . . . At the right moment I shall use all this to justify my action."

When the confessions of the two Englishmen did not produce sufficient evidence of Dutch official complicity, a special confession was drawn up in December, supposedly made by the dead Dutch lieutenant, to prove that plans for a revolution in Germany were supported by the Dutch General Staff.

The catastrophe that did not happen

We could not know all this on Friday, the day after the Venlo incident, when the German press suddenly fell silent. The warnings of an impending British landing on the Dutch coast and the attacks on the "suspect neutrality of certain neighboring countries" disappeared from the papers; judging by the press, peace seemed to have returned.

In Holland, on the contrary, Sas' warning was not being ignored as completely as he thought. On Thursday Holland's historic defense, the inundation of the centuries-old "waterline," an extensive north-south zone across the narrow center of the country, was put into effect and all military leaves were cancelled. Great emotion, general excitement! Was Holland in such immediate danger? Friday and Saturday were filled with tension and uncertainty.

On Sunday, November 12, the black day for which the attack was predicted, Holland waited under a dark and foggy sky for the catastrophe.

But nothing happened.

In Berlin that Sunday we were reeling with new questions. We could not understand why the attack had not taken place. Had the attempt on Hitler's life in Munich really been the work of the British Secret Service? Had Italy objected to an offensive against the Low Countries? Had the defensive preparations in Holland discouraged the attackers? Or, as some thought, was Sas the victim of a sophisticated plan to relay misinformation?

On Monday the Netherlands Prime Minister, a stubborn old gentleman who had amply proved his distrust of Sas' warnings, delivered a radio speech intended to reassure the nation. He just wanted to say that "the disturbing rumor of the last few days about an imminent danger of war for Holland lacked all foundation;" the government had been misinformed. He ended his speech by quoting a little Dutch poem which has since become famous in Holland:

> Man often suffers most from fear
> Of sufferance that may seem near
> But that in fact does not appear.

Former Prime Minister Colijn, who had called Sas hysterical, added insult to injury by declaring in an interview with Holland's biggest daily, *De Telegraaf:* "that he could very well guess what information the government had received, but that there had not even been a cloud in the sky." No wonder Sas had come back from The Hague like a beaten dog! I kept in touch with Sas for years after these events and always believed that these bitter experiences were something he could never overcome. At a most critical moment he had given his government invaluable information, which he considered absolutely reliable. It had been received with doubt and irony. Finally, when the planned attack had not materialized for reasons yet unknown, the government had publicly disavowed his information.

We know more now about why the offensive of November 12 was cancelled, or rather postponed. Here I will limit myself to the reasons we could assess at that time.

The main reason was undoubtedly the bad weather. The Rhine was unusually high. Gisevius, an anti-Nazi official of the Ministry of the Interior, wrote on November 8 that as he was driving through the countryside the fog was so thick that he could hardly find the road crossings. Obviously it would be mad to start an armored offensive under such conditions; and forecasts remained poor.*

A number of internal and international factors might have contributed. The German General Staff was very reluctant to start a winter offensive; even Goering was against it. So was Mussolini; although he would not have participated in military operations his feelings had to be considered. Finally, we hoped, the peace appeal of Queen Wilhelmina and King Leopold might have been a factor in the postponement.

All this was conjecture. Whatever the reasons, we now know that on Tuesday, November 7, at 13 hours, General Keitel, on Hitler's instructions, gave orders to stop the preparations for an offensive, probably until November 15. Ironically this was the very moment when our secret informer gave Sas the information—correct up to that minute—that the offensive would take place on the 12th.

* Hans B. Gisevius, *Bis zum bitteren Ende* (Zurich: Fretz und Wasmuth Verlag, 1946), quoted here from reprint by Ullstein Buecher, Frankfurt-Berlin, 1964, p. 219; English translation, *To the Bitter End* (Boston: Houghton Mifflin, 1947).

Five

THE WINTER OF NERVES

THE WAR SCARE of November 12 marked the beginning of a nerve-racking winter during which our Legation was startled almost every week by a new warning from Sas' informer. We learned after the war that Hitler postponed the offensive at least eighteen and perhaps as many as twenty-nine times, nearly always because of bad weather. But in that unforgettable long, gloomy winter, we never knew whether or when a warning would materialize. The experience of November 12 had, of course, aroused a good deal of doubt about the informer, even in our Legation. It is much easier for the human mind to face an immediate deadly danger than to stay ready for weeks and months for a danger that is both uncertain and invisible. There may be some truth in the little poem quoted by the Dutch Prime Minister, but the reverse is equally true:

> Most difficult we often find
> To maintain awareness in the mind
> Of a danger to which the eye is blind.

The mind then tries to protect itself either by shutting out the danger or by finding a reassuring explanation. The seemingly endless scores of warnings which followed but did not materialize certainly had this effect on us in the winter of 1939–40.

Each new warning Sas received from his "connection" was immediately transmitted by cypher to The Hague and through Sas' Belgian colleague Colonel Goethals to Brussels, where they survived the war in the form used in this book.

On November 22, 1939, the informer reported that in a meeting the previous day the attack had again been postponed temporarily, perhaps until December 3, perhaps *sine die*. He specified that December 3 was *mentioned*, but no *decision* to attack had been made. "I get the impression that they are in a deadlock," he added.*

A week later, on November 30, we cabled our government a report from Sas' informer that the offensive had now been postponed from December 3 to 10. However, if bad weather made another postponement necessary, the date might be December 25—Christmas!

The informer added that German intelligence had carefully studied the bridges over the Meuse and the parallel Juliana canal and the Dutch defense measures. They had concluded that the bridges could very easily be captured by pro-German infiltrators or fifth columnists. The informer strongly advised Sas to pass his information to the Dutch Supreme Command and to arrange for the

* van Welkenhuyzen, "Les Avertissements," p. 81.

bridges to be destroyed either on the spot or from a distance in case a bridge was captured by surprise.

On the other hand, he added, the Oberkommando der Wehrmacht had been impressed by the extent of the Dutch inundations. He recommended that these should be more widely publicized.

During the evening of December 7, 1939, Sas received another warning:

The date for the attack on the Netherlands has been postponed until December 17. Circumstances may lead to further delay, but it is certain to take place sooner or later. I know and understand that people may not believe me, but I swear that this is the truth.

In the O.K.W. it is believed that on December 17 the level of the natural inundations will have gone down enough; and Holland is swarming with spies who provide accurate observations.

The attack will take place with the help of units in Dutch uniforms, with armored units, and with paratroops.

Neither Holland's capacity nor its determination to defend itself is rated very high in Germany. It is assumed that attractive and shrewd offers can put an end to a resistance which, they believe, will be limited to the surface. One indication of this limited resistance is that the houses around the buildings destined for destruction in case of war have not been evacuated. These buildings will immediately be isolated by our Stukas [dive bombers] to prevent them from being destroyed.

Holland must do the impossible to defend itself against the inevitable attack.

I well remember how sick I felt after cyphering this message to The Hague. This was the most specific, the most ominous, and in retrospect the most accurate of the many warnings our Legation sent that winter. It made Holland's prospects look bleak indeed! Still we kept wondering whether we were the victims of a diabolic game.

The December 7 warning was not the last during 1939. On December 15 the informer reported that the decision would be put off until December 27. Hitler's Chief-of-Staff, General Alfred Jodl, had issued an instruction that on December 27 a decision would be made about the date of the attack, which would at the earliest be January 1, 1940.

And finally on December 27 Hitler decided—again to put off the decision until a big military meeting scheduled for January 9, 1940.

This series of postponements was, of course, grist for the nonbelievers. The events around November 12 had amply proven the skepticism of the Dutch government and the General Staff, and when nothing happened on that day they felt deceived. Their distrust of Sas' information increased greatly during the following weeks. Sas realized this with annoyance and on December 5 he again asked the Commander-in-Chief point-blank whether his information was being taken seriously.

He received a plain answer on his next visit to The Hague. During a stormy meeting, the General shouted, "God damn all this nonsense about you and your connection! I don't believe a word of it!"

The upshot was that Sas would be transferred from Berlin. This idea, however, was firmly opposed by the Minister in Berlin, Haersma de With, who continued to

believe in Sas' information in spite of its discrepancies
with events. The Minister refused to lose his most valuable source and insisted that Sas stay. Sas stayed, his
warnings continued, and they were less and less believed in The Hague. In the Military Intelligence Section's weekly reports they now appeared with a standard
warning that the source of the Military Attaché in Berlin
was not to be considered altogether reliable.

This did not change the Minister's view of Sas'
source. The Minister, a country squire, combined long
experience in international affairs with an almost
peasant-like shrewdness about human and political relations, and his experience in Berlin gave him a clear view
of the Nazi regime's ruthlessness and the violent antagonism it had generated within the German military establishment.

Furthermore, he had found that Sas' information was
often corroborated by other sources. One of these was
his friend Count Albrecht von Bernstorff, former Counselor of the German Embassy in London, who had been
thrown out of the diplomatic service because of his open
anti-Nazi attitude. At critical moments he came to visit
Haersma de With; and when we saw him walking
through the hall of the old-fashioned Chancery into the
Minister's office we knew: storm signal up!

Another source was "Jerry" van Maasdijk, reporter
and part-owner of Holland's biggest paper, *De Telegraaf,* who moved in Berlin's journalistic and society
circles and gained a lot of information. And one or two
officials at the Auswaertige Amt secretly sympathized

with our plight and gave us hints when the storm was drawing close again.

The best indication of danger, however, was on the wall of the Minister's office: a large staff map of Germany's Western border, on which Sas regularly indicated with colored pins the location of the German Army units. After the end of the Polish campaign the number of red pins increased, particularly between Aachen, near the southeast tip of the Netherlands, and Emmerich, where the Rhine enters the Netherlands. During the spring of 1940 the number of pins continued to increase ominously.

Haersma de With's attitude during those very difficult months, when he lived under the threat of invasion and accredited to a regime he despised, was the classic and, to my mind, correct one for an Ambassador. There was no doubt about his resentment of the Nazi regime, but in his opinion an Ambassador's duty was to foster good personal relations with the government to which he was accredited, no matter how much he disliked the regime. If an Ambassador could not do so, he should refuse the position rather than display his dislike under the protection of diplomatic immunity. I recall a remark the Minister once made to me before a luncheon he was giving for some Nazi leaders. As we walked to the dining room together he whispered, with his characteristic lisp: "Now I even have to feed the damned thcoundrels. I'd much rather poithon them!"

This undiplomatic sentence taught me a basic rule of diplomatic behavior: that one must show hospitality and courtesy towards the rulers of the receiving country, no matter what its regime—as long as the Ambassador makes it clear that he does not agree with the regime's principles or acts. If the Ambassador deliberately avoids or cuts off all personal connections, his own country as well as his compatriots in the receiving country only stand to lose.

Another good example of ambassadorial conduct in prewar Berlin was the French Ambassador, François-Poncet. He had excellent personal relations with Hitler, who appreciated him. Yet he consistently warned his government of the danger this fanatic presented to France and to Europe. He was in a position to do so precisely because of his firsthand knowledge of Hitler and his ideas. Nevertheless his warnings were as little heeded as those of Sas. In his memoirs he later characterized the reception of his warnings in Paris with the words, "People get used to gloomy predictions."

To clarify some of the events of that winter I must explain briefly the Dutch prewar neutrality policy and the very difficult position that resulted for us in Berlin.

Major Sas even then plainly condemned our neutrality as an "irresponsible house of cards" and postwar commentators have easily criticized it as shortsighted or foolish, saying that it was *obvious* that the Netherlands could not stay out of the war.

This is wisdom after the event. Indeed it is obvious *now*; that is why the Netherlands have since the war followed a policy of Western alliance and defense and of European unity. But it was by no means obvious in

1939–40. On the contrary, the Dutch nation, after 125 years of peace and neutrality, was largely convinced that we could again stay out of the war, provided we behaved with strict neutrality. It was even felt that our neutrality would be to Germany's advantage. Despite the strong resentment the Nazi regime had evoked within all Dutch political parties (except the small Dutch Nazi party), there was no disagreement with the broad outlines of the policy of neutrality. All our Foreign Ministers had, with the unanimous backing of their governments, adhered to it; Foreign Minister Eelco van Kleffens was acclaimed when he explained it once more in an impressive speech in Parliament soon after the outbreak of war.

Accepting neutrality, as the overwhelming majority of the Dutch did, meant that we had scrupulously to avoid any action that could be interpreted or exploited by one of the belligerents, particularly Nazi Germany, as contrary to our neutrality or as an excuse to attack. Several times early in the war both sides had tried to force neutral countries like Norway, Belgium, and the Netherlands to concessions the other side would certainly have considered a violation of neutrality. We knew that Nazi Foreign Minister von Ribbentrop had a special file in which all usable examples of non-neutral behavior were carefully collected.

For these reasons we had to adhere meticulously to an attitude of absolute neutrality, even when we in Berlin had little doubt about our country's impending fate. It required the utmost self-control to maintain that attitude day in, day out until the very last.

We now know that between the big alert of November 12, 1939 and the offensive on May 10, 1940 Hitler provisionally fixed the date for "Fall Gelb" at least nineteen times and postponed it eighteen times.* Each time Major Sas lost some of his credibility. This happened in part because people did not understand the informer's reports that a standby date for *preparedness* or for a *final decision* had temporarily been postponed. The final decision itself could still be rescinded until the last moment. In the later stages of war preparations this final decision need not be taken until a few days, and finally even a few hours ahead of the attack. Thus on November 7, but no later, Hitler could still decide to postpone the attack planned for November 12. To his anger he had noticed the elaborate defensive countermeasures being taken in Holland and Belgium that week. Hence he instructed that the time lapse between the order for preparedness and the order to attack, and between the order to attack and the actual moment of attack should be reduced to the absolute minimum. The time between the order to attack and the attack was gradually cut down to eight hours, greatly increasing the surprise element.†

This distinction between the orders for *preparedness* and those for the *attack* was never clearly understood in The Hague, partly perhaps because of Sas' own attitude.

---

* See de Jong, *Het Koninkrijk*, vol. 2, pp. 118, 123, 129; Jacobson, *Fall Gelb* (Wiesbaden: Franz Steiner Verlag, 1957) p. 141; Jean van Welkenhuyzen, "Het Alarm van Januari 1940 in Nederland" article in *Bijdragen tot de Geschiedenis van de Tweede Wereldoorlog*, p. 134, note 21.

† Hoffmann, *Widerstand*, p. 217; Generaloberst Halder, *Kriegstagebuch* (Stuttgart: W. Kohlhammer Verlag, 1962) Band I, p. 283.

Knowing that he was hardly believed in The Hague, he began to exaggerate. In practice this exaggeration only diminished his credibility more. This problem continued even after his enemy, General Reynders, was ousted as Commander-in-Chief in February and replaced by a general who was inclined to attach more importance to the secret informer.

The disaster threatening our country of course over-shadowed all personal considerations for those of us in Berlin. Nevertheless, many of us wondered what would happen to us then and what we could do to prepare for the worst. Most of us considered the alarm of November 12 a dress rehearsal. We now knew exactly what official records to destroy and what personal belongings to take along when the time came. More than preparing our suitcases we could not do; it was senseless and mentally impossible to live every day as if Armageddon were imminent. It seemed most likely that the Germans, with their enormous military power, would one day end the "phony war" with a blitz offensive, but its effect on the Netherlands' neutrality was less certain.

We continued to speculate on the role of Sas' secret informer. Since we knew that a fierce antagonism existed between Nazis and anti-Nazis, and that most old-school German career officers were in their hearts anti-Nazi, we could easily imagine that a high German officer, out of hatred for the regime, might give hints or even secret information to foreigners. In The Hague, as well as in Brussels and Paris, they were much more skeptical.

Some adhered to the theory of "the good traitor." They thought that the informer must be a German officer who, with the knowledge or even upon instruction of his superiors, was providing unreliable information to confuse the victims and lead them astray. In this view Sas was the dupe in a sophisticated "misinformation" plot and the unwilling instrument of an *agent provocateur*. This theory was compatible with the war of nerves Hitler had been waging successfully for years and was easy to accept in the nervous uncertainty that characterized that winter.

In an elaborate memorandum I weighed the evidence for and against the "good traitor" theory and concluded that it was not convincing. My paper did not seem to change opinions in The Hague. Yet I still cannot accept the harsh postwar judgment that the government in 1940 was unforgivably shortsighted not to believe the predictions of an attack. Now, in hindsight, the attack seems to have been inevitable. But not in those days. During the winter of 1939–40 there was good reason to doubt Sas' secret informer—at least until the invasion of Denmark and Norway in April 1940. Not thereafter.

An imminent offensive seemed even more unlikely because of the exceptionally severe winter, the coldest in 45 years. I got a personal taste of it during a New Year visit to The Hague, which also produced some unexpected observations.

We made such trips even in wartime because we had discovered that confidential documents sent by mail had arrived in Berlin opened or heavily damaged. In those days we did not have career couriers; classified mail was sent with trustworthy persons who were making the trip in any case. With the naïveté and confidence of an uninvolved nation, The Hague even sent some classified documents by registered mail. In Nazi Germany, where no letter was safe from prying eyes, this was utter madness, so we telephoned the responsible official in our Foreign Office to ask what had moved him to dispatch confidential documents *by mail*. He replied innocently, "But I sent it *registered* and besides the envelope had been sealed with the official seal." I don't think the good man ever understood the sarcastic laughter that greeted his remark. This small incident shows how little was known about Nazi methods by some officials in our Foreign Office—and by the rest of the country! At least it resulted in a ruling that classified documents should only be transported by trustworthy private couriers.

Thus all members of the Legation occasionally went as couriers to The Hague, a welcome escape from the nerve-racking atmosphere of wartime Berlin. Just before New Year I drove with my wife over the brand-new *Autobahn* to the Ruhr, and from there on small secondary roads to Holland. Not far from the Dutch border we met a huge military column in the gathering dusk. Leaders of the convoy frantically signalled us with red torches to move off the road, but I had lived long enough under the Nazis to know that one should only take no for an answer in cases of absolute necessity. I therefore shouted that I was on an official mission with important documents to be delivered that same night. This statement, loudly repeated and combined with the waving of my laissez-passer and my red diplomatic card bearing von Ribbentrop's signature, got us through. For more than half an hour our car jogged along the shoulder of the road, past an endless stream of tanks, armored cars, guns, and carriers, all with heavily dimmed lights, interspersed by shouting and swearing officers who tried to push us aside. Again the only remedy was flashing bright lights, loud and constant honking, and a big mouth shouting, "Official mission!"

As soon as we reached the Dutch border post I reported what I had seen and the customs officer promptly telephoned The Hague with my information. It was reassuring to note that our communication service was operating well. It was far less reassuring to wonder about the purpose of such an elaborate military maneuver along our border in the middle of an almost Siberian winter.

At least the weather would certainly discourage any military operations. As we crossed one of the big Dutch rivers I noticed that the engineers had placed elaborate tank barriers made from blocks of ice on the frozen river. Still later, around midnight, we were almost snowed in. Very late that night we celebrated the birth of 1940, with heavy hearts about what it would bring our country, but feeling that such weather would at least ensure quiet for a while.

That illusion was not to last very long.

The alarm of January 1940

On January 10, 1940 a small German Messerschmidt 108 aircraft got lost in a snowstorm on its way from

Muenster in central Germany to Cologne and made an emergency landing in Belgium near the river Meuse, right on the Dutch border. The pilot and his passenger were taken to a nearby military post for interrogation. The passenger was the German liaison staff officer of the paratroopers, Major Helmuth Reigenberger, who was carrying a heavy briefcase. During the interrogation he suddenly pulled some documents out of the briefcase and threw them into the stove. The Belgian interrogation officer, reacting as swiftly, pulled them out. The scorched documents proved to contain a complete plan for a German offensive extending from the Moselle River to the North Sea, including the airborne landing of a full division near Namur and an attack by the Sixth German Army from the Aachen area toward Maastricht, the Netherlands' southernmost city. The papers also included a survey of the Belgian forces in the area and a plan for occupying the Netherlands except for "fortress Holland," the western part of the country behind the "Water Line."

Such documents might seem completely convincing, but they were not. In Belgium they did cause great anxiety in a small circle of the initiated, once the King's influential Military Adviser had concluded that they were authentic. Both the French and Dutch Commanders-in-Chief, however, viewed them as unimportant. The French General, Maurice Gemelin, remarked in a staff meeting on January 12 that he doubted their authenticity, and General Reynders openly told the Belgian Military Attaché in The Hague, "I don't believe a word of it! Tomorrow I'll behave as if nothing has happened."*

Again the skeptics suspected a cunning German ruse; otherwise it was inconceivable for a German officer to be imprudent enough to fly over Belgian territory with a briefcase full of secret attack plans! The roots of their disbelief, however, went deeper. Many, including General Reynders, considered any German attack inconceivable because they believed the Germans wanted the Netherlands to stay neutral in order to maintain some transit trade through that country.

At that moment, indeed, the location of the German troops along the Western border did not indicate an immediate attack on Holland. The staff map in the Minister's office showed their placement as follow:

north of Emmerich (where the Rhine enters the Netherlands) only the First Cavalry Division and the Xth Army Corps;

from Emmerich southward to the parallel of Dusseldorf nine divisions, mostly reserves.

Only farther south did the concentration become more dense, numbering some 20 to 30 divisions down to Malmédy. †

The Netherlands Ministers for Foreign Affairs and Defense were less confident of our safety than the General Staff, and asked us in Berlin whether we knew anything about plans for an imminent attack.

---

* Testimony of General Diepenrijkx in *Bijdragen tot de Geschiedenis van de Tweede Wereldoorlog* (Brussels: Belgian Study Center for History of World War II, 1967), p. 131.
† van Welkenhuyzen, "Alarm," p. 132.

Sas could answer almost immediately. On Saturday, January 13, his informer had told him that Hitler was furious that his plans had fallen into Belgian hands and had decided to pounce immediately before proper defense measures could be taken. Consequently he had ordered the attack for the very next day, Sunday, January 14, at dawn.

As usual Sas gave this information to his Belgian colleague, who sent a cypher to Brussels—adding that he did not consider the information very reliable. Nevertheless, Belgian Foreign Minister Paul-Henri Spaak took the news seriously enough to summon the French Ambassador at 00:30 to give him this alarming information and request that *if* the attack should materialize, France and England should at once provide assistance in accordance with their declaration of 1937.

Since this time the first alarm had clearly come from Belgium, and Sas' informer had only confirmed it, even General Reynders could not very well ignore it. Therefore on Saturday night all Dutch troops were confined to quarters and all leaves were cancelled as of the next day. News of these measures caused a public emotion similar to that in November.

We in Berlin knew only what we had read in the telegrams from The Hague and its confirmation by our invisible informer. This was enough to shock us, but less than in November. One gets used to everything, even to the prospect of war.

Sunday, January 14, dawned an ice-cold wintry day. The wind had turned, allowing the fog to linger, and the watery sun that rose just before eight a.m. could not penetrate the heavy fog to reach the snow blanketing the Low Countries.

Again nothing happened. Again a false alarm! Were we still fooled by some scoundrel behind the scenes?

After the war we learned what had really happened. On January 10 the German meteorological service had predicted atmospheric disturbances on January 12 and 13, to be followed by 12 or 13 days of clear, cold, dry winter weather with good visibility and hard frozen soil: excellent conditions for airplanes and tanks.* In view of this favorable forecast, and to allow more preparation time, Hitler postponed the time of attack to Wednesday, January 17 at 07:36 Netherlands time, fifteen minutes before sunrise.

Sas' informer reported this postponement on the 14th, and we promptly sent a cypher to The Hague. But nothing happened on the 17th either.

The weather, one of the few elements in Nazi Germany that was not yet *gleichgeschaltet* (subject to Hitler's will), had fooled him again; on January 13 Hitler was obliged to postpone the attack for the umpteenth time, "probably until January 20." Then he began to receive news about cancelled leaves and other defensive measures in Holland and Belgium; obviously both countries had been alerted and were prepared. Even then Hitler hesitated to drop his pet idea of a winter attack. Giving it up would have implied that the General Staff

---

* Halder, *Kriegstagebuch*, p. 154; Jacobson, *Fall Felb*, p. 89.

had been right all along in advising against starting an offensive in the late fall or winter.

On January 15 Hermann Goering, General Keitel, and
General Halder met with General Jodl, Hitler's personal
Chief-of-Staff, in the O.K.W. to discuss the latest
weather forecast: no period of favorable weather would
be expected before February. To find a way out, Hitler
reverted to one of his earlier pronouncements, that
unless they could count on at least eight days of fine
weather, the offensive would have to be postponed until
spring. On January 16 he admitted it, though with great
reluctance. We received that news on January 19 and
sent a cypher to Holland saying that the offensive had
been postponed indefinitely.

After the January alarm came a period of apparent
quiet. We know now how deceptive this appearance
was. After the alarms of November and January and the
countermeasures they had caused in the Low Countries,
Hitler made a fundamental change in his plan of attack
and decided to occupy the whole of the Netherlands in
one sudden operation. On January 15 he ordered Goering to draft a plan for an airborne landing in the heart of
"fortress Holland," the urban area behind the "Water
Line."

But we learned this only after the war. During those
winter months of 1940 quiet seemed to have returned,
unbroken by new warnings from Sas' informer. He had
withdrawn from the stage, but only to prompt us from
behind the scenes.

On February 3 we sent The Hague his general estimate of the situation.

The Fuehrer's attention is still fixed on the Netherlands and Belgium. It has not been ruled out that something may be started if the weather should become favorable.

The secrecy has been tightened. I may not even be able to warn you in time. Apparently they are deliberately spreading reassuring news in order to lull the West into sleep.

Again we saw how hard it was for the human mind to stay alert to a lasting but invisible danger. Even in wartime Berlin, even in diplomatic circles, one often heard the theory that the "phony war" on the Western front would continue and finally fade into a tacitly agreed armistice. The theory's proponents argued that neither Hitler nor the Allies really wanted *this* war. France and England had declared war as loyal allies of Poland, and Hitler could say with some justification that Germany had never wanted war with *them*.

In late February I analyzed this idea that the phony war would peter out into a *de facto* armistice. I concluded that it was unlikely that the German General Staff or Hitler would sit back and wait for the enemy to give in or take the initiative to attack. The optimism in Berlin that winter was, in my opinion, wishful thinking. When I proudly presented my draft report to the Minister, I got an unexpected rap on the wrist. In his opinion it was not the responsibility of a Second Secretary to draft a political report on such an important subject. He added that his cook might as well start drafting political reports. My careful reply that a cook's task was to cook, whereas a young diplomat's task included political analysis, was not appreciated. My report remained in the archives and was burned in May.

At about that time we received some new intelligence from Sas' informer which strengthened my view. We cabled it to Holland on February 29, 1940:

> According to the usual informer it seems that new plans of operation are being studied, all of which have dropped the idea of achieving a surprise on one particular point of the West front. The aim is now a plan of attack with two main thrusts, one in the direction of Maastricht and one towards the hinge of the French and Luxemburg frontiers. These two main thrusts would be accompanied by offensive action along the whole front, extending in the North all the way to the North Sea at the mouth of the Ems river.
>
> The attack in the North would be carried out by the 8th or the 18th Army under command of General von Kluge, combined with a simultaneous maritime operation from the [German] island of Borkum towards [the Dutch naval base] den Helder skirting along the south side of the Frisian Islands.
>
> Up to now these are merely study plans; no decision has been taken or will be taken in the immediate future. Our informer thinks that such a decision cannot be expected until the beginning of April.*

Our impression of the informer's uncertainty was reinforced in his next message which we coded on March 21:

> I possess no concrete basis for an opinion. Secrecy is being tightened ever more. I have a feeling that nothing will happen

* van Welkenhuyzen "Les Advertissements," p. 130.

in the next two weeks, but in about four weeks an offensive might be launched in the West.

I repeat that, judging from pieces of conversation and from the attitude and thinking of staff officers, it will be a total offensive on the whole front, including Belgium and the Netherlands right up to the North Sea, with the main thrusts in the direction of Maastricht and of the hinge between the French and Luxemburg border. It will be supplemented by a naval action on the Dutch coast.

In the Netherlands the purpose would not only be to push back the Dutch forces but to annihilate them.

I do not believe in an attack on France alone, nor in a violation of Luxemburg only.

The tone has become more careful; the essence has remained the same.

The warnings from Sas' "connection" and others and the alert of January 14 were not the only signs of Germany's aggressive intentions during that eerie winter. German planes were flying regularly over Dutch territory. Their only purpose could be reconnaissance. But reconnaissance of what? For reconnaissance of France they need not fly over the Netherlands. For reconnaissance of England they would have to continue beyond our territory, which some did, taking the northern route over the Frisian Islands. But our observations showed that many others circulated only over the Netherlands.

These flights had started as early as September 1939, but increased in frequency after the end of October, coinciding with the first warnings of a German attack. After every violation of our air space we received a telegram from the Dutch Foreign Office giving the details and instructing us to ask for information or to protest if the facts warranted it. One of our diplomats then carried out the démarche, handing over a *note verbale* with all the details.

The officials at the Auswaertige Amt invariably promised an investigation, which just as invariably resulted after some time in a reply that no German planes had been in the neighborhood, so that it must either have been a plane of another belligerent (meaning British) or, as was plainly hinted several times, a Dutch plane! One German official demonstrated the Nazi mentality when he asked why we didn't shoot at the planes instead of protesting. Indeed, shooting at them would have been the only reply the Nazis would have understood, and which might have had some effect.

There were several reasons why we did not shoot. First, armed action was ruled out by our policy of strict neutrality. To maintain this neutrality, our government always made the same inquiries about violation of our air space *pro forma* simultaneously in London.

We had more compelling, practical reasons as well. The foreign planes had usually escaped before our slow fighters got on their tail; some of our long-stored AA ammunition was so defective that it could not reach the planes; and the oil of the fighters' machine guns froze at high altitudes.

During the night of February 20–21, 1940, the Luftwaffe had been particularly active. "Airplanes of unknown nationality" had been observed at seven different places over Dutch territory, though several of these observations seemed to concern one plane.

This time I was the lucky one to make the protest. To strengthen my case I asked and received permission to remind the Auswaertige Amt of all the previous violations. Hence I visited Legationsrat von Rintelen of the Political Section armed with two notes, one detailing the most recent incident and one recapitulating all violations since September 8, 1939.

Our own reports of these démarches, and the text of all our notes of protest were destroyed in May 1940, but my German counterpart's report of our conversation, written on February 24, has been preserved and published in the collected documents of the Auswaertige Amt.

Report by Legationsrat von Rintelen (Political Section).

The Secretary of the Netherlands Legation, de Beus, today handed me the attached *note verbale,* in which seven observations of German airplanes over Dutch territory on February 20 are taken as a basis for protest. In handing over the note Dr. de Beus added that it might in fact concern only two or three planes, because apparently several of the observations concerned one and the same plane.

In reply to the question formulated at the end of the note, whether the flights in the night of February 20–21 had been carried out by German planes, I answered Mr. de Beus immediately that I could now already state that they must have been British planes, since in the last few days we had received information about numerous flights by British planes over Dutch territory.

Subsequently Mr. de Beus handed me the second attached

note containing a list of all observations by the Netherlands military of supposedly German planes over Netherlands territory in the period from September 8, 1939 to February 3, 1940. Obviously the Netherlands Legation intends to maintain all its previous allegations about German flights over Dutch territory, notwithstanding our replies, which have nearly all been negative. Therefore I immediately told Mr. de Beus that the list was not correct, and that we had already stated our attitude on nearly all of these cases. Nevertheless I promised to check the whole list once more, which would undoubtedly result in a confirmation on our part of the incorrectness of these allegations.

With regard to the flight, denied in the same note, by a Netherlands plane over [the German border city] Nordhorn on January 14, I reaffirmed that the flight by a Dutch plane had been established beyond all doubt.

Rintelen

Von Rintelen's reply to me was undoubtedly in accordance with his instructions; otherwise he would not have lasted very long. But its truth is belied in the following note, also from the official publication of the Auswaertige Amt:

The documents contain many instances of reports by the Operations Section of the Luftwaffe to the Auswaertige Amt about flights of the German Air Force over Netherlands territory.

It is even more interesting to trace the origin of the Auswaertige Amt's official attitude on these flights to another document published in the same collection, a note by Vortragender Legationsrat Hewel, a personal aide to Hitler, on November 22, 1939:

The Reichsminister [von Ribbentrop] yesterday discussed with the Fuehrer the draft reply to the Dutch Government about the flights of German planes over Dutch territory. The Fuehrer instructed me to transmit the following guidelines:

1) In future all flights over neutral territory by German airplanes are to be *denied* categorically, unless they can be clearly proven, e.g. if the plane or some of its parts have fallen down or been found.

2) In these cases, where the overflight can be proven beyond doubt, the decision what to do is to be taken according to circumstances.

3) The Reichsminister requests Secretary of State Woermann to submit as soon as possible a detailed list of all the flights of German planes over the Netherlands and Belgium and a separate list of all such flights by enemy planes.

Hewel

Violations of sovereign territory have frequently been denied in diplomatic history, but rarely has one official document so cynically combined an instruction to deny all violations with a request for a complete list of these very violations.

Six

WESER EXERCISE

IN EARLY APRIL the relative calm we had enjoyed since the January alarm was rudely disturbed. Again Major Sas' informer gave us the first alarm. On April 2 we transmitted his warning:

It is an illusion to think that nothing will happen on the Western front. I am deeply convinced that the bomb will soon burst. I cannot give a specific date, but my personal impression is that April 15 could see the beginning of offensive action against Denmark in the direction of Norway, and three or four days later against Belgium and the Netherlands. I repeat that I am absolutely convinced of an impending offensive in the West.

As in his two last messages, he gave no precise dates, but his tone had become even more urgent. In retrospect the message also shows how well informed Sas' "connection" was; on that same afternoon Hitler had given the green light for the operation code-named "Weseruebung," or "Exercise on the River Weser."

This was our first hint of a possible attack on the Scandinavian countries. As military laymen we were surprised that the Germans would first launch an offensive against Denmark and Norway and then within a few days against the West. We had expected the opposite sequence; we had rather thought that in case of a Western offensive we would be exchanged via neutral Denmark. Since I knew Copenhagen well from my last posting, I had even asked permission to drive there one weekend and leave my car, which would at least save one of our possessions. Suddenly the whole picture was reversed! It was hard to believe.

More specific information soon dispelled our doubts. The next afternoon, Wednesday, April 3, Sas received from his friend the astounding news that Denmark and Norway would be occupied in the first half of the following week. Very soon afterwards the offensive in the West would be launched.* I remember vividly how Sas related his friend's announcement:

You may not believe me, but a large-scale expedition stands ready to occupy Denmark and Norway. The troops for Norway are now embarking in Swinemuende and Stettin. The occupation will take place next Tuesday (April 9). The offensive in the West will follow shortly. The operation is a personal initiative of the Fuehrer. It is being kept so secret that no one except the very top knows about it, in Germany at present not more than five other people. I am the sixth. It is of the utmost importance that Denmark, Norway, and England be warned. Do whatever you can!

* Testimony of Major-General Sas in *Netherlands Parliamentary Commission of Inquiry*, vol. I, p. 210; Heinz Hoehne, *Canaris, Patriot im Zwielicht* (Munich: Bertelsmann Verlag, 1976), p. 388.

Sas did what he could. In view of the serious situation our Minister had instructed that no code telegrams were to be sent out without his initials, so Sas could not send the warning immediately by cypher. But he had a secret arrangement with a friend on the General Staff in The Hague. In case of an expected German offensive, Sas would warn him by "inviting him to dinner" for a date one month *later* than the date of attack. So Sas called his friend in The Hague and invited him to dine in The Hague on May 9, thus warning him of the offensive expected on April 9. Unfortunately, since all telephone calls were tapped, he could not explain that the offensive was to begin in the North. This point was clarified by cypher the same evening:

Reliable source informs Military Attaché invasion of Denmark and Norway early next week certain, probably Tuesday. Great danger of offensive either simultaneously or shortly thereafter, against Netherlands, Belgium, and France.

Haersma

The warning to Norway

The next day, April 4, Sas went as usual to inform Colonel Goethals, who transmitted the warning to Brussels, adding his usual reservation about its reliability.

Then Sas set out to inform Norway and Denmark. In the bar of the Adlon Hotel, a popular hangout for diplomats and journalists, he found the Counselor of the Norwegian Legation, Stang, having lunch. When Sas asked his opinion of the military situation, Stang answered,

"That is not without danger; I hear the British will soon be landing in Norway."

Perplexed, Sas asked, "But don't you know that the *Germans* intend to land in Norway and Denmark on Tuesday?"

"Impossible!" exclaimed Stang. "That can't be true."

Sas replied, "That we shall see next Tuesday, and then you will know."*

Stang's expectation of a British landing in Norway was not entirely unfounded. His government had been deeply concerned for some time that England and France had been preparing operations in Norway to stop the flow of Swedish iron ore to Germany through the Norwegian port of Narvik. Churchill had openly spoken about these plans. They were changed when Finland was on March 12 obliged to lay down arms after its heroic "winter war" against the Soviet Union, but the French-British operations against Norway were still scheduled for April 5, and were only postponed until April 8 for technical reasons.

On the other hand the influential Norwegian Foreign Minister, Halvdan Koht, the Norwegian Navy, and the Norwegian Legation in Berlin were all convinced that a

---

* The exact content of the conversation between Sas and Stang has been the subject of much controversy and of an elaborate investigation in Norway by a Parliamentary Commission of Inquiry in 1945. Sas' account, as given here, differs from that given later by Stang, according to whom Sas did not specifically mention the coming attack on Norway. The evidence collected in the Norwegian Commission's Report leaves no doubt that Sas' account is correct. *Innstilling fra Undersøkelseskommisjonen av 1945* [Report of the Commission of Inquiry of 1945], published by the Storting [Norwegian Parliament], 1946, p. 144.

German attack on Norway by sea was politically unlikely and militarily impossible. Therefore, the Norwegian government considered the hints that Norway might be the target of the German ship and troop movements in the Baltic too vague to overcome their conviction that a German attack was highly improbable. The Norwegians were much more preoccupied with the manifest indications of impending English and French action against their country.* Stang's reply to Sas faithfully represented his government's concern about the Allied operations. But because Stang was a convinced Nazi sympathizer he did *not* faithfully transmit Sas' warning to his government.

The Norwegian Parliamentary Commission has published all the dispatches of the Norwegian Minister in Berlin, A. Scheel, to Oslo. In a strictly confidential letter of April 4, No. 638, the Minister reported on "European war; possible German push." This letter, drafted by Stang, states that a member of the Norwegian Legation had been informed by the Military Attaché of a neutral country of a reliable report that the Germans would march into Holland in the very near future, possibly in the next week. The letter then comments,

The Legation transmits the above with all possible reservations, but because it knows the Military Attaché concerned as a serious and well-informed man, the Legation does not want to fail to report on the subject.

The Military Attaché concerned also indicated a German

---

* Johs Andenaes, Olav Riste and Magne Skodvin, *Norway and the Second World War* (Oslo: Johan Grundt Tanum Forlag, 1966), p. 46.

invasion of Denmark with the purpose of procuring bases for German planes and U-boats on the west coast of Jutland.

A. Scheel

Not a word about the planned invasion of Norway, the main purpose of Sas' warning!*

That same afternoon, April 4, Stang visited the Counselor of the Netherlands Legation, Baron van Boetzelaer van Oosterhout. As the Baron, a very conscientious and careful man, declared later, Stang mentioned the rumors of an invasion of Norway and Denmark, adding that he did not take them seriously, because his German friends said the contrary. Boetzelaer, who knew that Stang frequented mainly Nazi circles, said that this did not seem a very convincing reason. He confirmed the news and insisted that the situation was "very dangerous and precarious" for Norway. †

The next day, Friday, April 5, something unusual occurred in Oslo. It might have set the Norwegian government thinking if they had received Sas' complete message in time.

The German Minister in Oslo, Dr. Curt Braeuer, invited a considerable number of Norwegian authorities to a reception and film showing at the Legation. Many Norwegians accepted, wishing to be correct to one of the main belligerents on whom their neutrality depended.

---

* Stang maintained later that he had drafted letter no. 638 exactly in conformity with the information received from Sas, but Sas confirmed later, on March 23, 1943, in London to Norwegian Minister Bentzon that he had certainly mentioned to Stang the coming German attack on Denmark *and Norway*.

† *Report of the Norwegian Commission of Inquiry of 1945*, p. 145.

The mood at the beginning of the evening was friendly and mutually polite. Braeuer could be a charming and hospitable host, as I knew from our social contacts in Brussels, where he had been Counselor. It was not by personal preference, but in compliance with a strict order from Berlin, that the film he showed later in that pleasant evening was *Feuerteufe* (*Christening by Fire*), a hair-raising documentary about the bombardment, siege, and destruction of Warsaw. Even in the dark one could feel the atmosphere slowly chilling as the peaceful Norwegians watched the ruthless destruction of the Polish capital and its screaming inhabitants perishing in the fire.

The spectators were aghast. Why was this film suddenly being shown here in Oslo, at this moment? Was this to show the model of the brave new Nazi world? More likely it was meant to intimidate the viewers with the military strength of the Third Reich and the futility of resistance. Yet even at that late moment, few realized fully why the film had been shown: that it was a warning not to resist Nazi Germany. The lights came on in painful silence and the guests hurried to take their leave.

One prominent Norwegian was conspicuously absent that evening: Vidkun Quisling, former Minister of Defense, who was known to have excellent relations in high Nazi circles in Berlin. Some of the guests wondered why he was not there; it seemed odd that he would miss an opportunity to fawn over the representative of the Third Reich.

Quisling had a very good reason for staying away: he

knew what was going to happen to Norway. In December he had twice visited Hitler, as well as the Commander-in-Chief of the German Navy, Grossadmiral Erich Raeder. He had largely convinced them that it would be to Germany's advantage to occupy Norway by surprise and put him, Quisling, in power as a reliable ally. Quisling's pleas had coincided with disturbing news in Berlin about England's planned landing in Norway. As a consequence Hitler ordered the O.K.W. to work out a contingency plan for the occupation of Denmark and landings in Norway; and on March 1 he issued his directive for operation "Weseruebung."[*] Although Quisling was not informed of the plan's final details, he knew that something of the sort was due.

In Berlin, Stang kept trying to hide the most disturbing news from his superiors. In the later afternoon of Sunday, April 7, Minister Scheel personally telephoned in cypher to Oslo his last warning, drafted by Stang in words designed to minimize the danger to Norway:

Noreg, Oslo.
66. It is learned from a trustworthy source that the troop transport of 15 to 20 ships with a total tonnage of 150,000 tons, mentioned in my report no. 611, has sailed from Stettin on a westerly course during the night of April 5. It is further learned that the port of destination, which is unknown, will be reached on April 11.

Scheel[†]

[*] Andenaes, *Norway*, p. 41; Brodersen, "Et Varsel fra Berlin", *Farmand*, Feb. 25, 1978, pp. 34 ff.
[†] Report of the Norwegian Commission of Inquiry of 1945, p. 52; Brodersen, "Varsel," p. 36.

Again, not a word about the imminent occupation of Denmark and Norway, which Sas had announced to Stang three days before! The only hint was that the fleet had sailed "on a westerly course" and would reach its destination only on April 11. But that was just as likely, perhaps more likely, to mean England or some other westerly destination such as Holland. (Stang later tried to explain this omission by saying that the reference to the earlier report, no. 611, implied possible action against Norway.)

In Oslo the officer on duty, Mrs. Gudrun Raeder, read the telegram over the phone to Foreign Minister Koht, who was at home. In view of the telegram's text it is hardly surprising that the Minister seemed undisturbed, feeling that it indicated an operation not against Norway but somewhere farther to the west. When Mrs. Raeder suggested that she send him the text by messenger he replied that it was not necessary. Like most of his colleagues, he still believed that the Germans wanted Denmark and Norway to remain neutral, as they had in World War I. He clung to this illusion until the last moment.

Early on Monday, April 8, the British Navy laid a minefield before the Norwegian port of Narvik. The indignant response in Norway seems to have overshadowed everything else that day, including a telegram from London warning that German naval forces had been sighted in the North Sea on their way to Narvik. Not until midnight, when the first report of German warships in Norwegian territorial waters reached the

Norwegian cabinet during an emergency session, did the government order the mobilization of *some* troops in specific areas of the country. Even then it stopped far short of general mobilization.*

That day, April 8, something else happened that clarifies the behavior of the German Minister, Dr. Braeuer. Many Norwegians must have wondered whether Braeuer knew why he had been ordered to show the film that threatened Norway with the fate in store for those who dared resist Nazi Germany. It is very likely that he did not. On that Monday, April 8, a certain Herr Pohlmann arrived from the Auswaertige Amt bringing a top secret sealed envelope for Dr. Braeuer with the instruction that he was to wait until 11 p.m. to open it. Always hospitable, Braeuer invited Herr Pohlmann to dinner, so he was present when Braeuer finally opened the sealed instruction.

"Never," Pohlmann stated later, "did I see anyone so surprised as Dr. Braeuer when he read the contents." No wonder the envoy was surprised: he was told to present to the Norwegian government the very next morning at 5:20 a.m., German summer time, an attached memorandum containing the demand not to resist the German landings then taking place.† This must have been the first he heard about the impending German invasion that night.

---

* Andenaes, *Norway*, pp. 48–49.
† *Nazi-Soviet Relations*, 1939–1941 (Department of State, 1948), p. 137. The Nazi machine worked like clockwork; at about the same time the German Ambassador in Moscow was instructed to hand over at 7 a.m. a copy of the memorandum to Norway and Denmark for information to Soviet Foreign Minister Molotov.

This was not the last of Braeuer's unpleasant tasks. Later, when the King and his cabinet escaped from Oslo, Braeuer was instructed to follow them into the mountains and convince them to end the Norwegian resistance. When this inevitably failed, Braeuer was sent to the front in disgrace.

The warning to Denmark: "Nonsense! Nonsense!"

On the afternoon of April 4, after his conversation with Stang, Sas visited the Danish Naval Attaché, who doubled as Military Attaché. He found Commander F. H. Kjølsen not entirely unprepared. When Sas dashed into his office, all excited about his news, he almost bumped into the Swedish Naval Attaché, Anders Forshell, who had just left the room, equally excited. It turned out that a high officer on the staff of the Kriegsmarine had told Forshell that an attack on Denmark and Norway would be made early in the following week, that the German troops were already embarking in Swindemuende, and that attacks on the Netherlands and Belgium would follow—all this in an obvious attempt to put Sweden at ease about its own security. The secret, which Sas' informer believed was only known to six people, had obviously also reached others. Several other Military Attachés had also heard about ship concentrations in Stettin and Swinemuende, and about a division of Alpine troops having arrived at Frohnau, north of Berlin. Alpine troops would hardly be needed in the heart of Germany except for dispatch to Alp-like snowbound territory elsewhere.

The Danish Naval Attaché recalled that early in Jan-

uary he had received a similar warning from the Greek
Naval Attaché, and in February from the Rumanian
Military Attaché. These less specific warnings mentioned an impending attack on Denmark and Norway to
be followed by one on the Low Countries. They show
that very early in 1940 foreign observers already had an
inkling of the plans.

The disturbing news about ship and troop concentrations in Baltic harbors had led Commander Kjølsen to
travel to Copenhagen on April 1 with a handwritten report from the Danish Minister in Berlin, Kammerherre
Zahle, which he took to the Foreign Minister, Dr. Edvard Munch, and to the Commander-in-Chief of the
Danish Navy.

After all the earlier warnings Kjølsen did not doubt
the information Sas brought him on April 4. They agreed
that Sas would inform Kjølsen by a code word if the final
decision was made and that Kjølsen would inform Sas if
Denmark decided to order mobilization, as seemed indicated. Kjølsen then hurried to the Danish Minister,
Zahle, with Sas' information. The Danes were even
more careful about their communications than we;
rather than use cypher telegrams for their most sensitive
dispatches, they sent the Secretary of their Legation to
Copenhagen, in order to hand the report personally to
Foreign Minister Munch and expound on it.

Munch received the warning late at night at home
but did not consider it important enough to receive the
Secretary personally. "The information seemed too

doubtful," he was to declare later. Actually, according to some witnesses, he even exclaimed, "Nonsense! Nonsense!"

On Friday, April 5, both Danish Minister Zahle and Naval Attaché Kjølsen in Berlin sent additional reports to Copenhagen, adding the news that crash courses in Scandinavian languages had been ordered for certain German police troops. Minister Zahle concluded this dispatch by warning "that the situation would become very serious within a few days."

The only result was that on Saturday, April 6, Secretary Schoen returned to Berlin with a letter from his Foreign Minister stating "that he could not see what military interest Germany could have in an operation against Denmark"—the same reason why so many in Norway and in Holland disbelieved the warnings.

On Sunday, April 7, the Danish Naval Attaché received two more clues. One from his American colleague, Commander Werner Schrader, said that troop transport ships had sailed from Swinemuende in a westerly direction. This was not new, but confirmed the earlier information.

The other, from Major Sas, contained only the agreed code words: "The order has been given."

These messages were immediately transmitted to Copenhagen, along with a final report from Minister Zahle in which he concluded "*that Denmark would very soon be faced with events without precedent in its history.*"

The warning to England

In The Hague, Foreign Minister van Kleffens believed that our carefully guarded neutrality would be violated if he, as Minister for Foreign Affairs of a neutral country, gave information about the military plans of one belligerent to its enemy. But without his knowledge the information had been secretly transmitted by GS III to the British Naval Attaché in The Hague, although in a much less specific form than the original. This is apparent from a coded telegram from the British Minister in The Hague to the Foreign Office in London on April 4:

The Naval Attaché [Vice Admiral Sir Gerald C. Dickens] was informed today by the Liaison Officer of the Netherlands Navy [Lt. Cmdr. C. Moolenburgh] that the Netherlands Admiralty is convinced that the Germans intend to launch an intensive propaganda campaign to intimidate the Nordic countries. They fear that this will be followed by energetic action against the Netherlands, Belgium, and Denmark, the latter country to be attacked first. The final action would include an offensive on the Western front.

The Liaison Officer added that a friendly source in Berlin has warned to be prepared for something serious next week.

The Director of Political Affairs of the Ministry of Foreign Affairs [Dr. J. H. van Roijen] has confirmed this confidentially in a conversation this afternoon with a member of my staff.

Bland

The most remarkable aspect of this telegram is the absence of the information most important to the British: the impending attack on Norway. Nor did the Danish and Norwegian governments warn England. This may help explain why England did not react much faster to the German attack. It would have been an ideal opportunity: the British Navy dominated the seas around Norway, it had that day laid a minefield in the approaches to Narvik, and two brigades and one battalion were already aboard ships in Scotland to counteract any German reaction to the minelaying.

That same Friday, April 5, another strange event took place in Berlin. The Supreme Army Command suddenly telephoned all Military, Naval, and Air Attachés to invite them for an inspection tour of the much-touted but very mysterious "Westwall" on Monday, April 8. They would depart on Sunday evening by special train and return Tuesday morning. The Westwall, a chain of hastily constructed fortresses along Germany's western border, was new and very secret. The opportunity was such a plum for military observers that they nearly all jumped at the invitation, overlooking its unusual informality. Only Sas and his Swedish colleague did not accept. Knowing what was about to happen, they saw through this diabolic trick. Later it was revealed that the order for the invitation came from Hitler himself, who wanted to get the unwanted foreign observers out of Berlin at this critical moment.

With us, the Dutch diplomats, the sensational news of the impending invasion had raised new doubts. Invasion of a weakly defended country like Denmark did not seem impossible; it had been whispered for some time that one day Germany might need to do it. "The occupation of Denmark is not a military problem, only an administrative one," Nazi officers had been heard to remark cynically. But Norway was quite a different kettle of fish—and the fish were, except on the Swedish side, entirely surrounded by water. A basic tenet of warfare is that one should never attack a country by sea if that sea is dominated by the enemy. And the North Sea *was* dominated by the British Navy, even though the British did not venture into the Kattegat, the sea arm between Norway and Denmark, where the Germans had air superiority. As the British Commander-in-Chief, General Sir Edmund Ironside, stated confidently, "The Admiralty is convinced that it can prevent any German landing on the west coast of Norway."

We knew that Hitler was by no means averse to risky, unconventional actions; but to invade Norway under the nose of the vastly superior British Navy seemed too foolhardy even for him. The German Army Command considered the operation a "mad enterprise." In the German Navy opinions were divided; Grossadmiral Raeder and the upper echelon were rather against such a risky plan, but many younger naval officers were enthusiastically in favor. They were inspired by the book *The Naval Strategy of the World War* by Vice-Admiral Wolfgang Wegener and a later memorandum by his son, both expounding the advantages to Germany of taking bases in Norway.* Thus it seemed possible that Hitler might risk the "mad enterprise."

To the few in our Legation who knew about Sas'

* Brodersen, "Varsel," p. 39.

warning, the long weekend dragged on in unbearable tension. Outwardly life went on as usual. My diary lists such trivial events as a farewell cocktail party for the First Secretary, a luncheon at the Legation, a lecture by a visiting Dutch professor, an antique auction, a dinner party at the famous Hoercher restaurant. Life seemed so deceptively normal that it was hard to believe that one of history's most daring military operations was even then being carried out. Soon we would know; this was the hour of truth for Sas and his informer.

On Tuesday morning I arrived at the Chancery at the usual time. There was no trace of excitement, no disturbing news in the papers, nothing special in the morning radio news.

"Poor Sas," we said to one another. "Now his informer's credibility is definitely finished. He might as well pack up." And we went on with our routine jobs.

Then, at half past ten, a radio talk about how much healthier life was without the (unavailable) coffee was interrupted by the usual "victory fanfare" reserved for important announcements. We froze.

"This is Reichssender Berlin calling.

"The Supreme Command of the Armed Forces announces today, April 9, 1940:

"In order to stop the British attack now being carried out on the neutrality of Denmark and Norway, the German forces have taken over the armed protection of these countries. To this end strong German forces have this morning entered Denmark and landed in Norway."

Like lightning the news flashed through the entire

Chancery: Denmark and Norway are occupied! Sas was right!

At almost the same moment the special luxury train with the Military Attachés, returning from their visit to the Westwall, pulled in at a reserved platform in Berlin. The gentlemen were cheerful; they had had an interesting trip, had been treated like princes in their luxurious sleeping cars, and had enjoyed the best food and wines available in wartime. Above all, their military problems had temporarily been reduced to speculation on how long the "phony war" would continue.

When the Danish and Norwegian Attachés stepped from their sleeper onto the red carpet, greatly relieved that the gloomy predictions about their countries apparently had not materialized, they were approached by a German officer. He very correctly clicked his heels, saluted smartly with a white-gloved hand, and informed them on behalf of the Reich Government that in view of a British attempt now being made to land in their countries, the German armed forces had been obliged to take over their protection. Of course the German forces came not as enemies but as friends and protectors in order to prevent horrible warfare in the Scandinavian countries.

The incredible had happened! Defying a classic principle of warfare, Hitler had occupied a country with troops transported over a sea dominated by the enemy. The surprise, the ruse, the foolhardiness had triumphed!

Later that day von Ribbentrop summoned all Chiefs of Mission to the new marble Reichskanzlei, a building designed to produce a maximum impression on official visitors. One entered a large marble hall and proceeded through a seemingly endless corridor, flanked on both sides by immobile SS men from Hitler's bodyguard. At the end we were kindly received in a sumptuous reception room and conducted to our seats by a protocol officer. When all were seated a door opposite opened and von Ribbentrop entered, followed by a horde of generals, party and government officials, all in ostentatious gala uniforms. In his usual harsh, arrogant tone, and with obvious satisfaction, von Ribbentrop read the Third Reich's official declaration why it had felt obliged to protect the two weak Scandinavian countries against the Allies' aggressive plans. We then all got a handshake and were dismissed. "A propaganda show to make you vomit," one of the Ambassadors mumbled, "and we are being used as puppets to dress it up!" The diplomats' lukewarm feelings for von Ribbentrop sank well below zero that day.

The success of the initial phase of Weser Exercise was awe inspiring. The Danish government, spurred to a speedy decision by German bombers droning overhead, capitulated at once in order to prevent useless bloodshed. In Norway the capital was taken by surprise the very first morning, as were Narvik, Trondheim, Bergen, and Kristiansand.

On the second day Sas' informer summarized his view of the operation in the north and its consequences for the West:

My personal feeling is that the offensive in the West will be launched in three or four days, depending on the further course of operations and on what the British will do. No decision has yet been taken.*

This message, carefully qualified as "personal feeling," was again correct originally but overtaken by events. In a meeting with General Halder on March 27 Hitler had indeed mentioned April 14 as a possible date for Fall Gelb, the attack in the West, but he had added that the final decision would depend on operations in Norway. After the first succèsses in the south, the occupation of Norway proceeded far less smoothly than Hitler had anticipated. King Haakon and his cabinet, with some troops, moved to the north, where the British landed and held out for two weeks at Trondheim. The German naval squadron was annihilated in two battles near Narvik and the city was occupied by the British.

These setbacks in the third week of April completely changed Berlin's feelings about the expedition: instead of an astounding success, it was now deemed a doubtful situation. No wonder Sas' friend told him on the sixth day:

The situation remains unclear. It seems that the British and French want to undertake action in the direction of Narvik. In the West nothing new noticeable. No concentrations either to the southeast. †

The setbacks in Norway delayed the plans for an immediate offensive in the West. This could and should

* van Welkenhuyzen, "Les Avertissements," p. 273.
† Ibid., pp. 378, 383, 384.

have given our country a last chance to reach a state of maximum military preparedness for the coming on-slaught. No one could now doubt that our source's information was both correct and important. From the time of Weser Exercise, we in Berlin no longer admitted any doubt about the authenticity of his information. In this conviction we cyphered his latest view to The Hague.

It was by no means received in the same spirit by the Dutch General Staff. Although all military leaves were cancelled on April 9, the Belgian Military Attaché in The Hague had reported to his government on April 5 that GS III "did not take Sas' information very seriously." Colonel Goethals, the Belgian Military Attaché in Berlin, transmitted Sas' warning with the notation that "it originated from the same informant who several times before made predictions with equal certainty which never materialized."* There is no sign that the amazingly correct prediction of Weser Exercise caused Sas' information to be taken any more seriously in Holland. On the contrary, when Sas next reported that the offensive in the West had been postponed for about a month because of bad weather and high water, whereas both looked rather favorable for operations, the staff at GS III openly called him a victim of the war of nerves.†

Even Sas' satisfaction about the cancellation of all Dutch military leaves on April 9 was soon overshadowed by two new blows from The Hague. The first was a letter

---

*Telegrams of Col. Goethals to Brussels of April 4 and 24, 1940.
†J. M. Somer, "Report on the events at General Headquarters during the days before the German invasion in the Netherlands" Internal report, London, April 2, 1943, p. 3.

from the Commander-in-Chief, reproaching him for not having followed the agreed code in his telephone conversation with his friend at Dutch headquarters. This had led to "measures and preparations which could otherwise have been avoided," meaning a big, unnecessary upheaval.

As mentioned before, Sas' invitation to dinner on May 9 had indicated that the offensive was to start on April 9, but he had been unable to explain over the phone that a preliminary attack on Denmark and Norway would precede the offensive in the West. The General Staff had understandably concluded that the attack *on Holland* was to take place on April 9. Thus Sas suffered a new setback in Holland just as his colleagues in Berlin were congratulating him on the "unique achievement" of his advance warning.

The second blow came from our Foreign Office. During the first week of April some officers of the Netherlands East Indies Army were on an official visit in Germany. Sas wondered whether they should not be informed that if Germany attacked Holland they would be cut off just when their country would need them most. We discussed this problem elaborately in the Legation and concluded unanimously that it was better to risk a premature and perhaps superfluous warning than the loss of several valuable officers at the most critical time. The officers were warned and hurried back to Holland. On these grounds the Foreign Minister berated Major Sas for having raised an untimely and unnecessary alarm.

On top of these signs of continued skepticism, the story reached us that our new First Secretary, before coming to Berlin, had been briefed not to cede to the atmosphere at the Legation, where "pessimism is dripping from the walls." These words, reported to us through the grapevine, flew through the Legation. They did not improve the morale of the staff members, all of whom were now convinced that Holland's turn was soon to come.

The staff map in the Minister's office confirmed our conviction. Ten divisions had been added along the German border with Holland, Belgium, and Luxemburg, five between Wesel (on the Rhine) and Aachen, and another five between Aachen and Trier. These brought the total along the Belgian-Luxemburg border to 68 divisions.*

In spite of all these signs, we were allowed almost a month's respite. On April 11 Sas gave us the following message from his informer, which we cyphered to The Hague:

The opinion at the O.K.W. tonight is that the situation in the north is not clear and may soon lead to a regrouping, especially of the Air Force. This would entail a postponement of the offensive in the West, which has, however, not been dropped.

On April 24 the informer approached Sas with this information:

The Fuehrer has written to Mussolini that he has decided to start operations in the West shortly. On the basis of my in-

---

* van Welkenhuyzen, "Avertissements," pp. 329, 332, 338.

formation and impressions I believe that an offensive could start next week.

The informer's news was not entirely correct; Hitler's letter to Mussolini did not mention an offensive in the West, and the setbacks in Norway had delayed any decision for an offensive in the week of April 29–May 5. The informer was, however, very near the truth, for at this point the war in Norway turned in favor of Germany and on April 27 General Jodl, Hitler's personal Chief-of-Staff, wrote in his diary, "The Fuehrer intends to start Fall Gelb between May 1 and 7."

The curtain was coming down on the northern theatre of war. The last act of the tragedy was about to open in the West.

Seven

THE LAST ACT: MAY 1940

The first day

FOR US IN BERLIN the last act of the drama started on Friday, May 3. As usual it began with an alarm from our bearer of ill tidings, who told Major Sas that afternoon, "General Keitel has personally informed me that the offensive in the West will soon start."

He advised Sas, however, not to report this information immediately to The Hague, where it would not be believed and would only arouse new irritation. It seemed wiser to wait and see what would happen next. Sas did, however, pass the news on to his colleague Colonel Goethals, who cabled it to Brussels, with his usual strong reservation about the reliability of the source.* As for The Hague, Sas decided to follow his friend's advice to wait and see.

He did not have to wait long.

The second day

The next day, Saturday, May 4, at around 2 p.m.,

* van Welkenhuyzen, "Avertissements," pp. 421, 445.

when I happened to be on duty at the Chancery, a long top-secret cypher arrived from our Foreign Office. From my slow decoding with the old-fashioned system of addition and subtraction there emerged the following message in which, for the first time, the Foreign Office sounded the alarm:

TOP SECRET

Barring intervention by a third power or unforeseen events, offensive is to be expected encompassing not only France, but also Belgium and the Netherlands, and possibly Switzerland.

Is anything about this known to Military Attaché?

We later learned that the warning came from the Vatican in a telegram sent on May 3 by Cardinal Maglione to the Papal Nuntius in Brussels and the Internuntius in The Hague. Pope Pius XII had received the news from Dr. Josef Mueller, secret representative at the Vatican of Admiral Canaris' resistance group. It was also revealed later that His Holiness had the moral courage to warn France and England on May 6. That day the British Ambassador to the Vatican reported to his government, "The Vatican expects a German offensive in the West to begin this week. But they had similar expectations before, so I do not attach particular faith to their present prediction. They say that it may include not only the Maginot Line and Holland and Belgium, but even Switzerland."

At the time we had no idea of the source of the Foreign Office's information, but we answered that it was completely confirmed by a warning our Military Attaché had received the previous day that an attack in the middle of the following week was very likely.

The third day

Sunday, May 5 brought a few confirmations; in fact they were no more than indirect indications, but those are the only pointers one has in such circumstances.

Major Sas received a telephone message from the Greek Military Attaché, Constantinides, prompted by disturbing German press items about tension in the Mediterranean. Much alarmed, the Greek had asked all his colleagues for information. The Japanese Attaché had answered that he had heard only that things would start popping in the West in a few days.

The Greek added a spicy detail: a Greek woman who was having an affair with a major of the Green Police (used outside the German borders) had reported that her lover had received the astounding order to report on May 12 at Headquarters of the Green Police—in Utrecht in the heart of the Netherlands! To outsiders this detail might have seemed insignificant, but we in Berlin had learned our lesson. A similar order had been received by a German police officer a few days before the invasion of Poland.

The fourth day

On Monday, May 6, the Legation received several bits of information confirming the earlier news. In addition, the changes on the staff map in the Minister's room were alarming. They showed this distribution of German troops along the Netherlands, Belgian, and Luxemburg borders:

from the North Sea to Emmerich	10 divisions
from Kleef to Roermond	9 divisions
from Roermond to Malmédy	28 to 29 divisions
from Malmédy to the Moselle	36 to 37 divisions

Some 73 German divisions concentrated on a sector of the front from Kleef in the north to the Moselle in the south—pretty heavy for "a purely defensive disposition" as Major Sas had been told.

On the other hand, the Belgian Embassy had heard that the big moment had not yet come because the ultimatum the Reich government intended to present to its victims was not ready.

That night, however, Sas' informer solemnly assured him that the attack on the Western front had now been fixed for Wednesday morning, May 8, at the break of dawn. The German forces had been moved into their jump-off positions, from which they could launch the offensive within twelve hours after the final order. Shortly before the offensive, an ultimatum would probably be served in the capitals concerned.

We immediately sent this news in code to The Hague. As usual, Sas wanted to inform his Belgian colleague, but since he had to remain available for further news from his informer, our Minister sent me to give the information to the Belgian Counselor, Vicomte de Berryer.

I called and asked whether I could come immediately on an urgent matter. In those days that could mean only one thing, so Berryer, who had already retired, told me to come along. The drive through the complete blackout was very slow, and it was almost midnight when I finally arrived.

Berryer, in pajamas and robe, listened to my story as he sipped a glass of whiskey. He did not seem particularly impressed, but nevertheless had found it worthwhile to ask the Belgian Military Attaché to come along. Neither gentleman hid his doubts about Sas' informer.

"Remember," said Berryer, "how often this man has told us"—and he boomed the German words in a heavy way—" '*Ich bin felsenfest ueberzeugt* . . . I am absolutely convinced that the attack is now going to take place!' But up to now his predictions have never come true."

"Except in Denmark and Norway," I interjected quickly.

My companions conceded that point, but reminded me that the informer had falsely predicted the attack in the West at least ten times. Of course such a warning should not be entirely neglected, so they would send it to Brussels the next morning, Tuesday.

Flabbergasted, I exclaimed, "But you're not going to lose a whole night! The attack will probably occur on Wednesday!"

Berryer, supported by Goethals, patiently explained his reasons.

"Look here, if we send this message *now*, one can

predict exactly what will happen. During the night they will immediately call a special cabinet session in Brussels. That cannot remain secret, so tomorrow all the papers will report it. Furthermore, the military leaves will probably be cancelled again. Imagine all the emotion, the excitement this will cause. And what if the attack does not materialize? Then we will look like idiots all over again!

"No, it's much wiser to send the news first thing in the morning. Then it can be handled discreetly without causing unnecessary commotion."

I pointed out that the Netherlands government had already been informed. But a Second Secretary could not prevail over two more senior and experienced officers; so they waited till morning, and Brussels did not receive their messages until 8:30 and 9:00 a.m.

By then the news was no longer new. The Dutch had already transmitted the information to Brussels through the Belgian Military Attaché in The Hague.

When, long after midnight, I returned home from my visit to Berryer, I telephoned Sas and in careful terms let him know that my message had been very skeptically received and would not be transmitted until early next morning. His response made me aware as never before of the Dutch language's rich vocabulary of swear words.

That same night, as I was visiting Berryer, another car was groping its way through blacked-out Berlin. The pitch dark hid the occupant, Legationsrat von Rintelen, the official who had received my protest against the German reconnaissance flights over Holland. He was a good friend of the Berryers, and like so many German officials had been torn between the instructions of his superiors and his personal feelings of friendship. This was to be his most difficult night.

He made somewhat faster headway through the darkness that I did because he was well acquainted with his destination: Wilhelmstrasse 73, the official residence of the Reichsminister for Foreign Affairs, Joachim von Ribbentrop, who had summoned him.

Von Rintelen was received by Chief-Aide Major Braun, who warned him ominously that he was to repeat nothing of what he was to hear. The Reichsminister made the threat even more explicit.

"You vouch with your head that no one is to know one word of the task I am to give you. Even towards my Secretary of State and the Under-Secretary you are bound to complete secrecy; those I shall inform myself."

The task was to draft on the spot the instruction the special couriers would carry to the Chiefs of Mission in The Hague, Brussels, and Luxemburg on May 7 or 8. The statement, which would be transmitted to the local Heads of State and governments, would justify the entry of the German forces. As a precaution, the couriers were to telephone Berlin for confirmation of their mission before leaving the Reich territory.*

Von Rintelen scrupulously respected the prescribed

---

* Information obtained from the memoirs of Mr. von Rintelen, kindly put at the disposal of the author.

secrecy, even toward his two superiors, von Weiszaecker and Woermann. Ribbentrop, however, did not keep his promise to inform them himself; he knew all too well that von Weiszaecker did not agree with his policy. As a result von Rintelen had an awkward time with his two superior officers, who took exception to his secrecy. But the order "You vouch with your head for secrecy" was no empty phrase in the Third Reich; it had to be taken literally.

Von Rintelen finished his gruesome task in an hour or two and went home with a heavy heart. He knew now that the die was cast; he had just produced it.

The fifth day

At about ten o'clock on Tuesday, May 7, the Auswaertige Amt telephoned an urgent request for diplomatic visas for four high-ranking German officials who had to leave for Holland immediately. Among them were Fritz Todt, Hitler's master builder, who had constructed many of the *Autobahnen;* Richard von Kuehlmann, known as one of the authors of the harsh peace of Brest-Litovsk, dictated to Soviet Russia in 1918; and a certain Mr. Kiewitz, who was described as "personal envoy of the Fuehrer in the Reich-chancery." Herr Hofrat Reimke stressed the urgency of the request; even over the telephone I could sense the nervousness of the Hofrat—who, judging by his title, must be a holdover from Imperial days.

I smelled a rat, and grew more suspicious when I learned that the gentlemen intended to *fly* to Holland— highly unusual in those days. The eve of a predicted attack seemed a significant moment for such a hasty trip by such high officials.

I told Herr Hofrat Reimke that unfortunately we could issue no visas without authorization from our Foreign Office, but that we would instantly apply for it. Then I consulted Counselor Bosch, who happened to be the top ranking official present.

Jonkheer Herbert Bosch van Drakesteyn was a scion of a noble Dutch family, married at that time to Nora Eastman of the Eastman Kodak empire. He had just relieved van Boetzelaer as Counselor in our Legation, but already disliked the Nazis as intensely as the rest of us did. For weeks we had been irritated by the way the Nazis consistently sabotaged or delayed our visa requests, while they themselves kept up a surprisingly elaborate courier traffic with their Legation in The Hague and always expected prompt attention to their requests. Now we had a chance to pay them back. More important, this was a rare opportunity to catch four fat Nazi fish in one net. We decided to delay the request as much as international practice would permit; in diplomatic language, "to deal with the matter in a dilatory fashion."

After some time I telephoned the German application to our Foreign Office, where it was received by Herman van Roijen (later Ambassador in Washington). I added that I would be on duty during lunchtime, so he could reach me at any moment; and I did not fail to remind him how difficult the Nazis had been recently in providing *us* with visas.

Hardly had I laid down the receiver when the

Belgian Military Attaché stormed into our chancery. Since our midnight meeting only twelve hours earlier, he had completely reversed his attitude. His skeptical calm had turned to nervous excitement. He appeared unannounced, deathly pale, and dashed straight into Sas' office.

What had brought about this complete change?

Ever since the Venlo affair we had suspected that von Ribbentrop had ordered someone in the Auswaertige Amt to compile a dossier with "proofs" of Dutch and Belgian nonneutral behavior towards Germany. A certain Dr. von Schmieden, guided by the legal counselor of the Auswaertige Amt, Dr. Gaus, was given the task. But von Ribbentrop reserved for himself the privilege of putting the finishing touches to the indictment and choosing the moment when it would be delivered in The Hague, Brussels, and Luxemburg.

The Belgians saw this dossier as the decisive indication of impending danger. That Tuesday morning, Dr. Auer in the Auswaertige Amt had hinted to Vicomte Berryer that von Ribbentrop had asked for the file "Ultimatum to the Netherlands and Belgium," and was preparing this document for delivery. To Goethals, this was the signal for imminent disaster. Now the roles were reversed, just as they had been in January; now *he* was the one who was convinced that our death knell—the German attack—had sounded.

This information made the German visa application seem even more suspect. During the lunch interval I got another telephone call from poor Hofrat Reimke, who obviously was being prodded by his superiors. Tongue in cheek and with some sadistic pleasure I explained at length how difficult and time-consuming it was to obtain a visa in wartime. Our own Legation had, to its dismay, experienced many long delays when applying for German visas.

That was understandable in normal cases, Herr Hofrat said, but in this case four very high Nazi officials on a special mission were involved. Their plane, so he inadvertently dropped, had been ready to take off for half an hour. I pricked up my ears at the news of a special plane standing by. Whatever their mission in Holland might be, we could only benefit from a delay in their departure. After consulting Bosch, I quickly drafted a cypher to our Foreign Office informing them of the Belgian warning and of the waiting plane. Before the telegram was ready, van Roijen rang to say that three of the visas were authorized, but more complete data was needed for the fourth.

Our new information and my consultation with Bosch led me to decide to withhold the visa somewhat longer. I told van Roijen, "You will first get new information from us. After sending it, I shall wait two hours before granting the visa, so that you can first take our message into consideration. If within two hours I have heard nothing to the contrary from you, I shall grant the visa."

Since the time was 14:15, in the absence of counterorders I would transmit the authorization to the Auswaertige Amt at 16:15.

But before then our department reacted—swiftly,

politely, and very effectively. I could assure the Auswaertige Amt that the high emissaries would be welcome in the Netherlands. They were, however, urgently
requested not to come by plane because all foreign
planes flying over Netherlands territory risked being
shot down. In view of the high rank of the emissaries,
the Netherlands government wanted to take every precaution for their safety and would therefore appreciate
being informed where and by what train they would arrive.

I have always remembered this message as a master-
piece of diplomacy because of its speed and politeness,
but only later did I fully realize how effective it was.

It certainly upset Hofrat Reimke. "That is a very
drastic decision!" he exclaimed.

It was indeed. Now the delegation could not possibly
according to plan reach The Hague before dawn on
Wednesday. Somewhat later we were told that Gesandter Kiewitz would leave by train on Wednesday at
12:43.

That tallied perfectly with Sas' new information that
the offensive would be postponed for one day but would
certainly take place before the end of the week. The informer added that we should watch for the arrival of a
certain Gesandter Kiewitz, who would probably carry a
message for Queen Wilhelmina and who would consequently be a harbinger of the attack. We coded this
news to The Hague on Tuesday evening.

In The Hague there was little sleep that night. They
were deeply disturbed by the three ominous reports

received within twelve hours: the warning from Sas' informer; the news that von Ribbentrop was working on the ultimatum to Holland, Belgium, and Luxemburg; and the sudden visa applications. All military leaves were again cancelled, new classes were called to arms, and defensive preparations were made. Understandably, all this aroused considerable fear and excitement in the population.

Even the diplomats betrayed this excitement. At 5 p.m. that day the Netherlands Minister in Brussels called at the Belgian Foreign Office. With unusual emotion the normally phlegmatic Baron van Harinxma thoe Slooten informed the Belgian government of the visa applications, their probable significance, the deep concern in The Hague, and added that the government had blocked all navigation.

As for me, in spite of the day's disturbances I went to sleep that night with a certain feeling of satisfaction. For Gesandter Kiewitz had not proceeded on his way to Holland. And neither had the German Army.

The sixth day

Wednesday, May 8, broke gray and gloomy—but again nothing happened. We could not know whether this was the one-day delay our informer had announced or another false alarm. During the first telephone contact with our Foreign Office that morning we inquired whether a plover had by any chance arrived to lay an egg. (*Kiewit* in Dutch means plover, and the finding of the first plover's egg in spring is a much heralded event, the egg being brought in triumph to the Queen.) They replied that no plover had been seen; it was probably too early for a plover's egg to be laid.

In spite of the inherent loss of credibility, Bosch and I rejoiced immensely over the new delay. Who knows, we joked, perhaps we had not only held back four Nazi emissaries, but also 75 German divisions! Not until later did we begin to think our joke might contain a grain of truth.

Later information established that Hitler had indeed intended to launch his offensive on May 8 and to have his emissaries hand over the ultimatum that morning in The Hague, Brussels, and Luxemburg in the hope of preventing all resistance. The emissary to The Hague was to be Gesandter Kiewitz, a hitherto unknown figure whom Hitler had selected specially for this mission. Three weeks earlier he had been summoned at one a.m. to come straight from his bed to von Ribbentrop, who informed him dramatically that he had been chosen for the highly important and deeply secret task of taking a message to Queen Wilhelmina of the Netherlands. The moment and the contents would be revealed later.

After nearly two weeks Kiewitz was summoned to Hitler's chancery. In the presence of Hitler and Goering he was ordered to stand by to leave for Holland the next day with a message for Queen Wilhelmina that would assure the "neutrality" of the Netherlands—after the first German bombs had been dropped.

When we prevented the Kiewitz group from flying to the Netherlands on Tuesday, we effectively delayed the plan von Ribbentrop had been preparing for months. To assure that in the meantime no word of the intended mission would leak out, the Nazi government then took a drastic measure only available to a totalitarian regime: the emissaries were simply locked up in the Chancery to await a decision on the future of their mission.

It didn't take place. Our delay of Kiewitz' group certainly contributed to the delay of the offensive, but it was hardly the main reason. Again, this was the bad weather forecast submitted to Hitler on May 7 at noon. With great reluctance the Fuehrer ordered General Keitel to postpone the order to attack on the 8th, adding that he would make a further decision at noon on the 8th.

The informer told Sas about the delay on the evening of the 7th. He suggested as causes "several unknown reasons, probably of a diplomatic nature, the strong attitude of the Netherlands and Belgium, and the delay in the departure of the diplomatic mission to The Hague."

On May 8 the weather forecast was not better. Hitler did not want to wait, but Goering insisted that his Luftwaffe must be absolutely sure of clear weather, particularly during the first days of operations. Furious, Hitler consented to one more day's delay—until May 10, "but not a day longer"—and Gesandter Kiewitz was kept locked up for another twenty-four hours.

The German press on May 8 continued to denounce English and American newspaper items about a coming German offensive as infamous lies meant to cover up for an intended *English* landing on the Dutch coast.

Major Sas considered these German press comments

a good reason to carry out an instruction from his Commander-in-Chief which he had so far held in abeyance. He paid an official call on the head of the Attaché Gruppe of the O.K.W. and explained to him that although we had no reason to expect a British landing, all necessary precautions had been taken to repulse any attempted landing. He added pointedly, "The Netherlands are fully capable of maintaining their own neutrality and do not need protection from whatever side." In view of events in Norway this statement was perfectly clear. The German officer answered politely that he would not fail to transmit the message to the competent authorities.

In the night of May 8–9, shortly after 2 a.m., the telephone rang in the London home of Paul Rijkens, Dutch President of the Unilever concern. It was Mr. Davies, a Liberal M.P., who said that he was with Winston Churchill and Lord Beaverbrook, who had both received indications from the United States that the Germans would invade Holland that very night. The Foreign Office had said they knew nothing about it. Could Rijkens find out?

Rijkens called the Dutch Minister in London, Jonkheer Michiels van Verduynen. This gentleman was "not pleased" to be disturbed in the middle of the night, as Rijkens tactfully wrote in his memoirs. Michiels said that he could hardly imagine that he would not have been warned if something serious were afoot, but since important personages were inquiring he would call the

Dutch Foreign Office in The Hague.

The telephone there was answered by the sleepy voice of a well-known and well-liked junior official in the Personnel Department who was on night duty and sleeping on a folding cot next to the telephone.

"What, are *you* the duty officer?" Michiels exclaimed. He was obviously surprised that a much more senior official was not on duty during those critical days. Without mentioning who had inquired he put his question.

As no new messages had come in during his time on duty, the young man answered truthfully, "Everything is quiet, Sir, there is nothing happening."

Michiels promptly called Rijkens back and said with some irritation, "I've just had our Foreign Office on the phone. Everything is quiet; nothing is happening. They don't understand where you got that story!"*

The seventh day

The morning of Thursday, May 9, passed without new developments. It was an anticlimax after the excitement of the previous days, and as we went through the files selecting the most urgent papers for burning, we again began to doubt the imminence of the offensive.

Early in the afternoon Sas' informer gave him a message, which we immediately cyphered to The Hague:

This afternoon Hitler has fixed the launching of the offensive on the whole Netherlands-Belgium-Luxemburg front on

---

* Paul Rijkens, *Handel en Wandel*, and information provided by the duty officer, Mr. Bart Fledderus, to the author.

May 10 at the break of dawn. The order can still be rescinded, but not later than 21 hours tonight.

The news gained credibility because the weather was clearly improving. In addition the political weather in the West was very favorable for a German attack: in France the Reynaud Cabinet had resigned over the position of General Maurice Gamelin, and in England Neville Chamberlain was on the verge of offering his government's resignation. There is no definite proof that these favorable political conditions influenced Hitler; as we have seen, his decisions were above all determined by the weather, and his long wait was rewarded by weeks of the most beautiful weather he could have wished for his campaign. But the political disarray among the Western democracies undoubtedly helped his plans succeed.

I do not remember exactly when the informer's message came through, but we must already have been alerted during the afternoon because my wife and I wondered whether to go to the dinner party of our friend Don Heath, First Secretary and at that moment Chargé d'affaires of the U.S. The Minister and his wife had a similar problem; they had been invited to the gala première of the opera "Cavour" in honor of the visiting Italian Foreign Minister, Count Ciano. This was to be followed by a small reception at the home of the Horstmanns, a society couple who kept the last salon surviving in Nazi Berlin. After much consultation, the Minister decided that it would be contrary to our neutral policy to cancel these engagements at the last minute. This would create the impression that we were expecting the worst, which was still not 100 percent certain and should in any case be concealed from outsiders.

Eight

THE EVE OF WAR

OUR INFORMER'S MESSAGE left little hope. But although orders had been given and Hitler had left for the West front "to place himself personally at the head of his troops," the order might still be rescinded until 9:30 at the very latest. If no counterorders were issued by then, the informer said, "Then it is definitely the end."

Sas and his friend dined together in town that last evening. This was hardly prudent, but prudence was not in their natures. It was a depressing last meal; their only satisfaction was that no one suspected either of them.

At nearly 21:30 they took a taxi to the Oberkommando der Wehrmacht on the Tirpitzufer. The German jumped out and disappeared into the somber gray building, leaving Sas to wait outside. The twenty minutes he spent there, he told me later, were like waiting for a death sentence. He knew the outcome, but even a man condemned to death will hope until the last minute for a miracle or for a stay of execution.

This time the execution was not stayed. When the informer emerged again from the darkness between the pillars he clutched Sas' arm and whispered with hardly controlled emotion, "My dearest friend, this is really the end. No counterorders have been given. The swine has left for the West front. This is really and definitely the end." The code word "Danzig" had been given out at 21:45. The offensive was on.

The farewells of the conspirators were emotional. For months they had risked their lives to stem this offensive. Now the fate so long predicted would befall Holland, Belgium, Luxemburg, and France. The friends promised to meet again after the war—perhaps even in the summer of 1940: the Nazi leaders had ordered triumphal arches for August.

Sas raced back to the Dutch Chancery, where he had asked the Belgian Military Attaché to wait for him. Time was short. From the attacks on Poland, Denmark, and Norway we knew that at a certain moment all telephone and telegraph communications between the victim country and its Legation would be cut off. Anticipating this, Sas realized that cyphering the final alarm would take too long. As soon as he arrived at the Legation he grabbed the telephone and asked for an urgent priority call to The Hague. It took twenty agonizing minutes before the call came through, twenty minutes during which the connection could be cut off at any moment.

At 22:35 Berlin time, the Naval Aide to the Dutch Minister of Defense, Lieutenant Commander Post Uyterweer, came on the line. Without preamble Sas shouted, "Post, you know my voice, I am Sas in Berlin. I have only one thing to say: Tomorrow at dawn! Hold tight! Will you please repeat? You understand what I mean, of course."

Post Uyterweer carefully repeated the message, then added, "So letter 210 is received?"

"Yes, letter 210 received."

These code words, agreed upon earlier, meant that the invasion (200) would take place on the 10th.

Another last supper of peace

In the meantime my wife and I had dutifully gone to the black-tie dinner of the American Chargé d'affaires, First Secretary of Embassy Donald R. Heath, in his duplex apartment at Innsbrueckerstrasse 44. His superior, Alexander Kirk, had left for a few days' holiday in Switzerland, so our good friend Don, although only a First Secretary, was temporarily in charge.

Much as we liked Don and his wife Louisa, the dinner was sheer torture for us, notwithstanding the excellent food and the interesting guests. One of those, I remember, was Dr. Abs, then the youngest Director of the Reichsbank, who was to play a big role in the German banking world after the war.

The minutes crept by. The beautifully prepared dishes nauseated me. Conversation moved haltingly over the usual topics of wartime Berlin—the wonderful new car, the Volkswagen, which the Nazis had just produced; food distribution and the resultant headaches; the chances of a compromise peace in the West— wouldn't it be foolish to start a war there that no one wanted?

In the middle of the meal I was called to the telephone. Could I come to the Chancery immediately to help cyphering? I could return to the dinner later. The voice on the other end left little doubt that the message to be coded was the final one.

I excused myself profusely with our host and hostess. In my car I groped my way through the Berlin black-out to the Rauchstrasse, reminiscing about the events of the last seven months leading up to this moment.

At the Chancery I found almost the entire diplomatic staff assembled, including Minister Haersma. Very little was being said.

"Is it certain?" I asked.

"Irrevocably certain," said Sas. "Look, could you put this in cypher as quickly as possible?"

He pushed a paper into my hand, and I read:

Information from connection Military Attaché; beginning of offensive tomorrow at break of dawn. According to him absolutely certain.

Haersma

The words "according to him" still retained a remnant of doubt and reserve.

I cyphered the text as quickly as I could. It was dictated over the telephone, the fastest way as long as we had the connection.

We soon received a return call from The Hague. It was Lieutenant Colonel van de Plassche of GS III, who asked with obvious doubt "whether the operation was completely certain, and whether Sas had consulted all doctors."

Sas, furious at this unnecesary exposure to discovery in open conversation, snapped back, "Yes! I don't understand why you are still bothering me! That operation is irrevocable. I have consulted all doctors. Tomorrow morning early, at dawn, it will take place." He slammed down the receiver.

At the other end of the line Colonel van de Plassche put down the receiver and sighed, "Now they've gone completely nuts."*

In Berlin we stood in silence. It was finished. Sas had performed his last duty as Military Attaché.

"There is no stopping now anymore," he said, pondering the events he had set in motion. "Now the bridges will be blown up. That was the intention of my connection."

Sas' informer had always been concerned about the three main bridges over the Meuse at Maastricht and two at Roermond, as well as five out of fourteen bridges over the Juliana Canal parallel to the Meuse. He knew what he was talking about because the Abwehr had the task of capturing the canal bridges with special forces in Dutch uniforms. However, Sas was too optimistic: in fact the bridges were not all blown up before the attack. All the Meuse bridges at Maastricht and Roermond were destroyed by the Dutch after initial fighting, but those over the Juliana Canal were taken by surprise by *Abwehrtrupps*, thanks to their disguise in Dutch uniforms—and thanks to the Dutch failure fully to heed the informer's warning. Had *all* the bridges been blown up,

* Somer, "Events at General Headquarters," p. 5.

the central German thrust through the Low Countries would at least have been hampered, though probably not enough to make a decisive difference.*

At the Minister's urging, Major Sas went back to his hotel to fetch his nightgear and spent the night at the Legation, a wise precaution for his safety.

At the Chancery some others resumed the task of burning secret papers, which would keep the chimney smoking until dawn. I retured to my dinner party, having obtained the Minister's permission to tell Heath what was going to happen.

Don Heath opened the door himself and we had a brief, subdued conversation in the entrance hall.

"What's the news?"

"Awful," I said, my voice strangled. "Tomorrow at dawn, an offensive on the entire front. France, Luxemburg, Belgium, and Holland. If things move badly, perhaps even Switzerland."

"I am deeply sorry for your people," Don said. "We must join the other guests for a little while, then may I come with you to visit Haersma? After that I'll try to call President Roosevelt personally. I hope for God's sake that my country will at last realize on which side it should stand."

"I hope no bad news?" Abs asked when we joined the party.

"Well, nowadays no news is ever good," I said, as casually as I could.

My wife and I took our leave as soon as protocol per-

* de Jong, *Het Koninkrijk*, vol. 2, pp. 427 ff.; vol. 3, pp. 66 ff.

mitted, but we waited downstairs for Heath to guide him through the blackout to our Chancery. There he received the Minister's confirmation of the bad news, then drove straight to the U.S. Embassy, where he asked for an urgent personal call to President Roosevelt and arranged for Mr. Kirk to be intercepted on the night train to Basel.

Once contacted, Alexander Kirk left the train before it reached Basel. But the call to President Roosevelt did not go through. The German operator explained that all telephone communication with foreign countries had been cut off. . . .

We stayed at the Chancery for a short while to burn classified papers.

Later, at our house in Grunewald, my wife and I began the tasks we had rehearsed so often. We would let our child sleep until the last minute. The poor creature would have a difficult enough time being dragged through warring Europe—where to? For the umpteenth time we brought out the suitcases and began to pack.

I switched on the Dutch radio and heard, to my surprise, the Central Air Control Bureau. In a flat bureaucratic tone, as if he were reading the weather forecast, the reporter was repeating at brief intervals, "Great numbers of foreign planes of unknown nationality are crossing the eastern border of our northern provinces in a west to southwesterly direction."

Somewhat later the "great numbers" had grown to "hundreds of foreign planes of unknown nationality."

Many who heard these announcements still thought

that the aim was an attack on England. They did not know that the German bombers had instructions to fly as far as the North Sea, then turn around and attack Holland from the west.

We in Berlin did not know the details either. But we knew the intention of these "planes of unknown nationality" and our fears were soon to be confirmed.

In Holland the irony of history continued to the last. At half past three in the morning Foreign Minister van Kleffens, in a telephone conversation with the Netherlands Minister in Brussels, still denied any massive overflights. Almost half an hour later he received a request through the same channel: "Couldn't we please stop those announcements of the Air Control Service; people in Brussels get so frightfully nervous over them!"

Van Kleffens transmitted the request to his colleague in Defense, Dyxhoorn, who called the duty officer of the Central Air Control Bureau to relay the message to him. Halfway through his request, another telephone in the room rang. The rest of his conversation was superfluous: the "planes of unknown nationality" had dropped their first bombs on Rotterdam airport at 3:55 in the morning.*

The ultimatum

The Nazi war machine worked with frightening precision. In Berlin, exactly five minutes before the first bombs were to be dropped on Holland, Minister van Haersma de With was awakened by Legationsrat

* de Jong, *Het Koninkrijk*, vol. 2, p. 455.

Wagner of the Auswaertige Amt. Could the Minister come as soon as possible to see Foreign Minister von Ribbentrop? He added that he had seen to it, that a car was already waiting in front of the Legation.

At ten minutes past six, when the attack had been going on for more than an hour, Haersma was received by von Ribbentrop. The reception was icy. For months, we knew, von Ribbentrop had been compiling a file of so-called violations of neutrality by Belgium and Holland. On this basis, he had on Tuesday finalized a memorandum ending with an ultimatum not to offer resistance. This memorandum should have been carried to The Hague by Gesandter Kiewitz; we had prevented this by sabotaging his visa application.

Von Ribbentrop now handed this memorandum to the Netherlands Minister. It consisted of a long list of accusations purporting to prove that the English and French were planning to launch an attack on the industrial Ruhr area through Holland and with Holland's assistance.

The Minister indignantly refuted all these accusations. There was no question of a British attack on our country, he said, but even if it should occur we would be perfectly capable of resisting it. The Netherlands had scrupulously maintained its neutrality, as every impartial observer would testify.

Von Ribbentrop stated coldly that he had other information at his disposal. The Venlo incident had proven that the British Secret Service, with the help of high Dutch officials, had planned a coup against the Fuehrer and the Reich government. He also knew from very reliable sources that since Wednesday evening, the 8th, troops had been standing by in England for a landing in Holland. (A remarkable piece of foresight, since he had prepared the memorandum on the 7th.)

Then, in standard totalitarian fashion, von Ribbentrop presented the carrot or the stick—a pretty big carrot and an even bigger stick. He urged the Dutch government to be as wise as the Danish and not to offer useless resistance. In that case the Third Reich would guarantee our independence, the retention of our overseas territories, and the continuation of the dynasty. (Apparently von Ribbentrop had been briefed that these would be the three concessions most appealing to the Dutch.) If, on the other hand, we were foolish enough to resist, Holland would be utterly destroyed.

Although telephone communications with Holland had been cut off, von Ribbentrop continued, he had arranged for a special line to The Hague in the adjoining room so that the Dutch Minister could transmit the message to his government.

Accompanied by State Secretary Gaus, Haersma went to make the call, hoping to gain time as he did so. But the Dutch had beaten the Nazis to the draw: the connection had been cut off on the Dutch side.

After long and futile attempts to get a connection, Haersma returned to von Ribbentrop. He remained standing to speak his last words to the Nazi Minister: "I have not been able to get the communication with The Hague. I have nothing to add to my statement that the

Netherlands will resist to the utmost. Germany alone will bear the responsibility in history for this unprovoked aggression against a friendly country." Von Ribbentrop replied, "I can only say that I feel sorry for the Netherlands if they intend to resist."*

I was awakened that morning by a terse telephone message from the First Secretary: "It has happened. The Minister has been summoned by von Ribbentrop."

Instinctively I went to the Rauchstrasse, where Haersma had just arrived. He told us briefly about his meeting with von Ribbentrop. Actually we had nothing to do but to await our fate, whatever it would be. In the early morning of May 10, as the tragedy of Western Europe began, the prelude in Berlin came to an end. The center of events had moved to the battlefield; suddenly our Legation's role had ceased. The diplomat's duty is to prevent war, or at least to delay it, but once the guns raise their voice, that of the diplomats becomes inaudible and useless.

Our only remaining task was the traditional "asking for our passports." Now that diplomatic relations had come to an end, we must request the German government to allow the Mission and its staff to leave the country. Members of the Legation staff differed on how to proceed. Some felt we should submit only a formal note asking to leave the country; others held that this scandalous attack on a friendly and neutral country demanded a strong protest.

*Netherlands Parliamentary Commission of Inquiry, vol. IIa and b, app. 60, p. 132.

Haersma de With was a careful and thoughtful man. He pointed out that the main thing was to get out of Germany. Of course diplomatic practice entitled us to do so, but the Nazis had shown several times, as in the occupation of Czechoslovakia, that they felt no obligation to comply with this practice if it did not suit them.

Most of our other staff members, especially the younger ones, favored including a sharp protest. After months of bearing Nazi intrigues and arrogance, we felt no further need to be polite. To our great satisfaction we obtained permission to draft a note which, even after forty years, seems to me worth quoting at least in part.

The note began with the statement that German armed forces had without notification attacked the Netherlands. Since the Netherlands were now in a state of war with Germany, the Minister asked for exit passports for himself and the Legation staff, as well as for all the non-German members of their families and households. The note continued:

The German aggression against the Netherlands lacks even the slightest justification. The Netherlands have scrupulously adhered to their neutrality, which the German Chancellor had several times solemnly promised to respect, lastly on August 26, 1939. They have refrained from military contact with any other country. They have done nothing to which an honest and impartial observer could take exception, and they were firmly determined to defend their neutrality on whatever side necessary. The Netherlands have always tried to work for peace, as was proven once again by the mediation offer of H.M. the Queen, together with H.M. the King of the Belgians, in November 1939.

Germany has, in violation of the most elementary principles of law and morality, torn to pieces the centuries-old bonds of peace and friendship with the peoples of the Netherlands.

The German aggression will not fail to shock deeply the conscience of the world. The German Reich will bear the exclusive responsibility toward history for this deed.

At 3 p.m. our Counselor Bosch handed this note of protest to Legationsrat von Halem, Deputy Chief of Protocol at the Auswaertige Amt.

Our careful Minister, whom we had that morning considered a bit too careful, proved to be right: at eight that evening Bosch was summoned to the Auswaertige Amt. First he was kept waiting, but he was in no mood to accept such treatment. He sent in a message that if he were not received immediately, he would return to the Legation.

The Nazis understood such language, and within moments Bosch was shown into von Halem's office, where an approximation of the following dialogue took place:

von Halem: "I have instructions to return the note which you transmitted this morning, because it constitutes an insult towards the Reich government."

Bosch, naively: "What does the Reich government object to?"

von Halem: "Herr Aussenminister von Ribbentrop has personally taken exception to the next to last paragraph, and in particular to the words 'the German aggression.'"

Bosch: "But I don't see what other expression one could use in this case."

von Halem: "There is no question of aggression!"

Bosch: "What would you call it?"

von Halem: "We are not talking about that now. Please have a new note drawn up, requesting your passports without further comment."

Bosch returned to the Legation, note in hand. But he couldn't hide his satisfaction as he said, "But they *have* read it all the same. And they even kept the copy!"*

A new note was drawn up, but never handed over. When it was ready the Swedish Legation, which had been put in charge of Dutch interests, told us that the Auswaertige Amt no longer wanted it.

Thus despite eight months of Sas' persistent and precise warnings, Hitler's massive offensive on the Western front on May 10, 1940 still came as a surprise. It seems unlikely that the offensive could have been prevented or defeated if the Western governments had heeded Sas' warnings. Hitler was determined to deliver a knockout blow in the West before turning East and his war machine was too powerful for the Allies at that moment. But his military operations would have been far more difficult and perhaps not always successful if some action had been taken:

• if the British government had received Sas' warning of April 4 in full and had immediately intercepted the German convoys to Norway;

---

* This has been confirmed by the publication of the refused note in the series of documents of the Auswaertige Amt. *Akten zur Deutschen Auswaertigen Politik*, Serie D., Band IX, Zweiter Band, p. 256.

• if the Norwegian and Danish governments had, upon receipt of that same warning, taken immediate defensive measures;

• if the Dutch and Belgians had in time closed the gap between their defense lines, which Sas' messages repeatedly mentioned as a primary German target;

• if they had informed France in advance that in case of a German attack they would request French troops to be sent north up to the mouths of the big Dutch rivers;

• if, after Sas' final warning, they had blown up all strategic bridges over the Meuse and the Juliana Canal and blocked all airfields.

Nine

AFTERMATH

ON THE DAY of the attack, Friday, May 10, we were surprised to find that our freedom of movement was not at all restricted. Thus we could finish packing and dispose of whatever furniture a few of us had brought to Berlin. Being one of these unfortunate few, I arranged for a Berlin moving firm to store our furniture, including many lovingly collected antiques, in the Legation. (That turned out to be a mistake. Three years later I learned from the Swedish Legation, which looked after our interests, that the Netherlands Legation had been hit and burned to the ground in one of the big Allied bombardments in November 1943. Ironically, the old house in Grunewald from which I had evacuated the furniture remained undamaged. . . .)

After the dramatic events that climaxed in the night of May 9–10 a feeling of complete helplessness and uselessness suddenly overcame us. All winter and spring we had been kept going by the tension, the excitement, the new developments, and the fascination of collecting and dispatching secret information. Now all this had suddenly come to an end. We wandered through the Chancery not knowing what to do, like a family that has tried for months to save the life of a beloved member and then feels utter emptiness when the loved one dies.

Many of our compatriots crowded the lobby of the Chancery to ask for help and advice. It was heartbreaking to have to say that we could no longer do anything for them. We were ourselves prisoners, privileged only in that we *hoped* to be allowed to leave the country. But even that proved uncertain.

On Saturday, May 11, we received a message from the Auswaertige Amt that we were all to assemble at the Legation before 10 p.m. We were to bring our suitcases and we were not to leave the Legation again, in reprisal for the internment of the staff of the German Legation in The Hague at the Hôtel des Indes.

The Residence at Rauchstrasse 10 was an old-fashioned gray house built in the ornate style of the early twentieth century, when Berlin experienced its greatest expansion. The Chancery was housed in the old annex at the back. The Residence could house a few guests in addition to the Minister's family and servants, but it was a far cry from the luxurious Hôtel des Indes and was definitely not designed to house the thirty-six staff members who suddenly found themselves within its walls. We made the best of it. Everyone was asked to provide his own linens and blankets; the largest rooms were evacuated and transformed into dormitories. Since there were, of course, no thirty-six beds in the house, most of us slept on the floor. Major Sas happened to be bedded down next to us, and early the following morning I was awakened by my three-year-old daughter, who whispered, "Daddy, I just stepped on the little Major. Is that bad? I think he is already sleeping again."

The Nazis were not in the least concerned about how to feed us. We soon heard that the Nazi Chief of Protocol, von Doernberg, who had often dined at the Legation, had said, "Don't worry, at the Dutch Legation they have plenty of good food and drink; I know that from experience."

That we had, but not in quantities to feed thirty-six people at each meal. Fortunately kind friends at other Embassies helped. The Americans and Brazilians in particular proved to be real friends. They visited us regularly and provided our only permitted contact with the outside world. In front of the Legation a *Schupo* (policeman) and a hefty, athletic figure, obviously a Gestapo man in mufti, patrolled day and night. The 8mm film I secretly made of that episode of our internment shows our jailers patrolling back and forth before the gate.

While we had no real material problems, the uncertainty of not knowing our fate was hard to bear. From our diplomatic visitors we heard that the Swedish Legation was still trying to get us exit permits, but no decision had been taken yet. As usual in a totalitarian regime, no one dared make a decision except the dictator himself.

On the fourth day after the attack we were informed that in expectation of the decision we would be transferred by special train to a hotel on the Swiss border, where we would be interned. Each person was allowed only two suitcases.

And what then? we asked.

That was in the hands of the Fuehrer, was the answer.

At lunch our Minister made an emotional appeal that in these difficult circumstances we should above all behave with dignity.

We did. But we did not respect the two-suitcase limitation. International law obliged the Nazis to let us depart with a normal amount of luggage; if they wanted to hold some of it back they would have to be responsible for it. Fortunately they didn't. At the indicated hour we were fetched by bus; a truck followed for the luggage. Preceded by a police car with screaming sirens, we drove for the last time through the familiar streets of Berlin. We were not to see the city again until years later—in ruins.

A special train was waiting for us; the platform had been sealed off from the public. The only others there were faithful friends from a few other Embassies who had the courage to show their sympathy by their presence. The train moved out slowly amid waves and tears. It was the saddest farewell a diplomat can experience: to see his mission ended by war.

The Auswaertige Amt had sent with us Legationsrat Zapp, previously Secretary of the German Legation in The Hague. He took great pains to make our trip as bearable as possible. After the war, when his own fate was at stake, I was happy to testify that he had been most helpful. However, he could not hide from us the presence on the train of a considerable number of hefty "gentlemen" who kept a watchful eye on us and on the doors of the sleeping cars.

We had agreed that we would accept only the un-desired Nazi hospitality necessary to remain alive, so we did eat the dinner we were served in the diner, but refused the wines and liqueurs offered in profusion. We were greatly surprised to hear next morning at breakfast that every drop of drink had been finished. I made it clear to Zapp that none of it had gone down Dutch throats. Apparently the Gestapo had thoroughly enjoyed it.

Our group was interned in Friederichshafen on the Lake of Constanz in the Kurgartenhotel, a very comfort-able establishment with a lovely location and a beautiful view of the lake. Normally these would have been very pleasant holiday surroundings. But it was a gilded cage, and the birds didn't know whether they were ever to regain their freedom. International law prescribes that if war breaks out the diplomatic missions of the two sides are exchanged. But we arrived in Friederichshafen to hear the shocking news that Holland had capitulated after the bombardment of Rotterdam. What? How could that have happened? But it was true. And since our en-tire country was occupied by the Germans, from the German point of view the war with Holland was over.

For us, this meant that the members of the German Legation interned in the Hôtel des Indes in The Hague must now be free. Since we no longer had a counterpart for which we could be exchanged, we were completely at the mercy of the Nazi government, and we had often enough seen what that meant. Perhaps they would respect the diplomatic tradition and let us depart. But they might well take the position that after Holland's occupation we no longer represented an independent country and had become private citizens who simply had to go back to our own country. At the outbreak of the war the English and French diplomats had been exchanged via the Netherlands. I had personally, on behalf of our Minister, bade the official farewell to French Ambassador Coulondre and his staff when their diplomatic train left for Holland. I remember telling the French Secretary that I hoped we would meet again, and his cocky reply: "We will, when I come back to Berlin after our victory."

The French and British diplomats had been exchanged, but they held German missions in their capitals as counterparts, whereas we had lost ours. On the other hand, when the Nazis had occupied Czechoslovakia, we had never heard from the Czech diplomats again. Our concern about the Nazis' decision was not unfounded; later, when Yugoslavia was attacked, its diplomats disappeared in a concentration camp.

We also worried about whether the Nazis had discovered the many secret messages the Legation had received and transmitted to The Hague. We had been careful to burn all incriminating papers at the Legation in Berlin, but they might not have had time to do it at the Foreign Office in The Hague when the Germans moved in.

Of course our greatest fear in this area was for Sas. His last open warning over the telephone, "Tomorrow at dawn!" must certainly have been heard; surely the Nazis were on his track.

This conversation, we learned later, had indeed been tapped and reported to the Abwehr, where it reached Count Michael Soltikov. With the consent of his chief, Admiral Canaris, he managed to make the report disappear and so saved Sas and his informer—temporarily.*

In addition to these personal concerns, we had good reason to view the future with gloom during those distressing idle days. Via Sweden we had asked the Netherlands government, which had taken refuge in London, for instructions. But no answer could change the hard facts: Holland was occupied and every day brought new reports of German victories on the Western front, reports which were soon confirmed by the Western stations we received on our little clandestine radio.

The most devastating news after the capitulation of Holland was the completely unexpected announcement over the German radio, preceded by the usual victory fanfare: "The French Maginot Line has been pierced near Sedan over a width of 100 kilometers."

The impregnable Maginot Line had been broken? Could that be true? But then, it had only taken the Germans a few hours to capture the "impenetrable" fortress of Eben-Emael near Liège. Nothing and no one could resist this war machine. It was not only the Poles; in the West similar tragedies were occurring every day. And if

* van Welkenhuyzen, "Les Avertissements," p. 550.

the Nazis won this war and imposed their dictatorship on the whole of Europe, what then? In those days it was hard for me to believe that life would still have any meaning.

I also wondered what I could do as an expatriate for my occupied country. I was convinced that even the super-efficient Nazi war machine could be beaten; for in the end man will always rally on the side of freedom and the word is stronger than the sword. Our nation's most pressing need in the dark years ahead would be a clear concept of what we were fighting for, what future we would aim for if we regained our freedom, what values of the past we would wish to retain, and what reforms we would want to introduce. On the back of a menu of the Kurgartenhotel I began to draft a pamphlet which was later published in London under the title "Rebirth of the Kingdom." Two copies were smuggled via Sweden into Holland and there copied, reprinted and stencilled manifold by the Dutch underground press. The pamphlet, which started a discussion in Holland about our postwar political system, was one of hundreds of such efforts, all over Europe. They showed that the spark of the free word could inspire resistance to oppression and helped conquer it in the end.

Early in our internment we heard from the Swedish Legation in Berlin that they were still trying to get our exit permits, strongly supported by neutral major powers such as the United States and Brazil, but they had no definite answer for us.

After about a week, we received two answers. One

was from the evacuated Dutch government in London, instructing the permanent civil servants to leave Germany and remain ready to be summoned to London if necessary. Those not in permanent government service were free to choose either to go abroad or to return to Holland.

Juridically this was perfectly logical. The government and its permanent civil servants were firmly committed to each other; besides, the civil servants were bound by their oath to the Queen, who had moved to London with her government. Athough no such ties existed between the government and the temporary employees, these were angered by the government's refusal to take a firm commitment to them. They considered this attitude a breach of faith toward citizens who had suffered just as much for their country as had the permanent staff.

Feelings were not improved by the decision from Berlin, which arrived soon afterwards. Briefly, it said that the Netherlands were occupied and the war between the Netherlands and Germany had ended therewith. Nevertheless, the Fuehrer, in his great magnanimity, was giving us a choice: *either* we could go back to Holland and dedicate ourselves to the peaceful reconstruction of our country, *or* we could leave for Switzerland. Those who chose Switzerland would never again be allowed to return to Holland.

Clearly the Nazis considered this a magnanimous offer; and since they assumed that Nazi-Germany would soon win the war, they expected us to choose the path of wisdom and return to Holland. They were astonished and almost indignant when we all chose freedom. They could not understand this "shortsighted" preference for a completely uncertain expatriate's existence over return to a country now at peace under Nazi protection. They stood by their word, however, and made all preparations for our departure while we lived until the last moment in fear of a counterorder from Berlin.

On May 20 at noon we embarked on the ferry that would carry us across Lake Constanz to Switzerland. Half an hour later we sailed into a little harbor on the Swiss shore. Romanshorn was its name. None of us had ever heard of it, but never has the Swiss flag been greeted with greater relief and emotion than the one flying on the pier of Romanshorn. We were really free!

Late in the afternoon we arrived in Bern. At the railway station we were greeted by a tall, slender young man in perfect diplomatic outfit: navy-blue pinstriped suit, black coat, and homburg hat. It was our young attaché in Bern, Mr. Joseph Luns.

In the subsequent weeks the members of the Berlin Legation were summoned in turn to London by our government in exile. My turn came in early June. My wife and child, a secretary, and I first traveled from Bern to Paris as the only passengers on a sleeper train, which to my surprise was still running normally even as the decisive battles of the war were being fought on the Somme. Just as the wheels of society need a long time to get going again after a war, so they go on turning for a surprisingly long time unless they are directly disrupted by the violence of war.

In Paris the picture was far less peaceful; the night
before the Germans had bombed a factory in the Paris
region for the first time. Nervousness had gripped the
population and a stream of refugees began leaving the
capital. We were put up in a little hotel, the Montalem-
bert, which also housed our small improvised Military
Mission to Allied Headquarters, under the command of
a major I had known at our Legation in Brussels. Since I
had for weeks been without reliable information about
the war, I asked him to tell me plainly what the military
situation was. He took me to his office, where the floor
was covered with large staff maps of northern France,
and gave me a detailed exposé. I don't remember the details, but I do remember all the more his devastating
conclusion: "From a military point of view, the matter is
decided."

At that moment many in France were still hoping
that the miracle of the Battle of the Marne in 1914 would
repeat itself, but the ensuing days proved the major's
conclusion only too correct. Hitler won the Battle of the
Somme and the rest of France lay open for him, which
meant that the fall of Paris could only be a matter of
days. Therefore we were greatly relieved to learn from
the Legation that they had been able to book us provisionally on the last ship due to sail for England in about a
week's time from St. Malo in Normandy—"if any sailings
should still be possible next week." They advised us
strongly to leave for St. Malo immediately in order not to
get stuck in Paris and overtaken by the advancing German army. We needed no encouragement; as soon as

possible we fought our way onto one of the westbound trains crowded with hundreds of refugees.

St. Malo felt to me like Friederichshafen: another gilded cage—a lovely hotel, a beautiful beach, glorious weather, lobster galore. But every day the French war communiqué became more gloomy; the French government evacuated to Bordeaux; the Germans entered Paris; Paul Reynaud made his dramatic "last appeal" to America—and no ship arrived from England. The last remaining clerk at the shipping agency offhandedly said that he could not guarantee that the ship would come at all. But *if* it came and *if* it sailed, then one thing he could guarantee: it would be the last crossing—one way.

After almost a week the ship *did* come—and we fought our way on board before it sailed out of the harbor of St. Malo that night, without lights, but toward the light of freedom.

Farewell to Sas: cocktails with bombs

London in June showed little surface evidence of the war: no air raids, no rationing, restaurants and movie houses crowded, everything plentiful, even gasoline. Only the big silver blimps floating over London and the trenches being dug across St. James Park recalled that we were living in wartime.

Though London was still physically untouched by war in those days before the Battle of Britain, it was crowded with exiles from all over Europe. Hence I was pleasantly surprised to find a nice little penthouse with a roof terrace on a narrow street in the heart of London bearing the romantic name of Petit France (pronounced Petty France) and within walking distance of Stratton House on Piccadilly, the Dutch government headquarters. Only weeks later, when shell splinters pierced the windows, did I realize that this glass house, pleasant in peacetime, was definitely not the safest place to live under aerial dogfights and bombardments.

In July the attacks by Goering's Luftwaffe began. At first they were not directed against London but against the shipping in the Channel, the harbors, airbases, and other military targets along the south coast. The intention was to engage the Royal Air Force in battle and eliminate it gradually, so that in September "Operation Sealion," the invasion of England, might take place. When the Luftwaffe started its big offensive on August 10, 1940, it had 4,295 fighters available against the RAF's 704. This 6 to 1 numerical advantage did not deter the British pilots. From our roof terrace we had a fascinating grandstand view of these heroic, uneven dogfights. Sometimes announced by an air raid siren, but as often without warning, little dots of enemy planes would come into view over the London skyline, slowly getting closer, until they were swooped upon by the British Spitfires and Hurricanes. Circling each other like fighting dogs, they drew silver streaks through the pale blue summer sky. The Battle of Britain was on.

In London we found nearly all the diplomatic members of our Berlin Legation. Our reunion with Sas was the most emotional moment. It was clear, however, that he was still bitter. After all that had happened he had expected at least an appreciative reception from the government, thanks for all the warnings he had passed on, and an open admission that they had been wrong to doubt him. But not at all! There were too many of the doubters in London and they received Sas with cool formality. Sas was not a man to hide his resentment at this treatment and soon became somewhat isolated.

There was one exception, as Sas told me with great emotion. He had been invited to one of the small informal luncheons Queen Wilhelmina sometimes gave for young Dutchmen who had risked their lives to escape from occupied Holland to join the war effort in England. At the end of the lunch the Queen rose and made a short speech. She said she wanted to pay homage to a man who had not received the great honor he deserved from our country, Major Sas. She wished now to express her respect to him and apologize that not enough credence had been given to all his warnings from Berlin. This was one of those thoughtful and truly royal gestures that made Queen Wilhelmina a mother to her country.

To relieve Sas of his difficult position in London, he was slated to leave early in September for Canada, where he would recruit and train new Dutch forces overseas.

We decided to give a farewell cocktail party for Sas and his wife. The unforgettable experiences we had shared had forged a strong bond of friendship between us, and besides he had rendered invaluable services which in my opinion had not been sufficiently appreciated. Rarely in history has any country been kept so consistently and accurately informed from day to day about an impending attack. Rarely, too, some commented bitterly, had any government paid so little heed to these warnings.*

My wife and I invited all the ex-Berliners to the party, which we planned for the last Saturday before Sas' departure. We would hold the party on our roof terrace if the weather was good.

The weather cooperated; Goering did not. Towards 5 p.m. the sirens started wailing. In that phase of the war these attacks rarely lasted more than half an hour or an hour, so we figured that even if our guests did not leave home until after the "all clear" they might still arrive without too much delay.

But this attack seemed different from the usual hit-and-run fighter raids; it sounded much heavier and closer by. We heard one wave of planes after the other, the heavy drone of the Junker bombers followed by unusually strong explosions. Soon large black clouds of smoke started to rise above the East End. These seemed to act as beacons for ever new waves of planes; the black clouds soon began to show a red glow on the underside.

After more than an hour, the sirens wailed the "all clear." From the roof terrace we saw a terrible sight. The entire eastern part of London seemed to be on fire, be-

* This is not quite true. There have been at least two similar cases where a government received and simply refused to believe such precise advance information about a coming attack: the warnings of the super-spy Richard Sorge about the impending Nazi attack on the Soviet Union, and the information provided by Cicero, butler of the British Ambassador in Turkey, about the Allied invasion-plan in 1944.

decked by one huge black layer of smoke. We could hear the fire engines and ambulances screaming through the streets, all in the same direction—to the burning docks.

Our guests began to arrive. In their shelters they had not been able to witness the attack, but now instead of enjoying cocktails, we all stood silently watching the docks of London burn. That day's fires were the biggest conflagration since London's great fire of 1666.

We did not know then that a few days earlier Goering had ordered his two Air Force commanders to launch the big air attack on London "and to continue until the RAF would have destroyed itself in useless attempts to stop us." That Saturday, September 7, was the beginning of the Luftwaffe's massive attack. That day 372 German bombers and 642 fighters began their gruesome task.

It was a dramatic farewell to Major Sas, in keeping with the dramatic experiences we had shared with him and with his turbulent life. His career during the rest of the war continued to be interspersed with conflicts with government authorities. Nevertheless after the war he was appointed Head of the Netherlands Military Mission in Washington with the rank of Major-General. At last a happier and more satisfying future seemed to be awaiting him. But fate continued to pursue him. On his way to Washington he died in a plane crash—a tragic and explosive end to a tragic and explosive life.

Ten

THE INVISIBLE INFORMER

SAS LEFT LONDON that autumn still guarding the secret of his informer's identity; we learned no more until the end of the war. Our only clue, his stunning advance warning about the attack on Denmark and Norway and later about the offensive in the West, showed us that the informer must rank high in the German military establishment to have access to such secret information. Now it is time to reveal the identity of this ghost who for seven months had dominated our lives.

Colonel Hans Oster, son of a Lutheran minister, 52 years old, possessed all the best qualities of the old-school Prussian guards officer. He was a man of great physical and moral courage, thin but athletically built, strikingly handsome despite his pale complexion. He always wore a monocle, and was as successful with women as with horses.

His valor in battle had twice earned him the Iron Cross in World War I. He considered himself bound for life by his oath of allegiance, sworn as a young officer to Emperor William II; his affection for the Netherlands stemmed from our refusal in 1919 to extradite the fugitive Emperor after he had sought political asylum in Holland.

Oster's charm with women likewise earned him many victories, but brought his career on the General Staff to an untimely end when, in 1932, he was found to be carrying on a passionate love affair with the wife of one of his superior officers. Under the strict standards of the old German officer corps this was an unforgivable offense that obliged him to resign his commission.

Yet even those rigid rules had loopholes. Soon after the scandal, with the support of General Halder, Oster was appointed to a modest position in the German counterintelligence service, the Abwehr. Because of his low position there he was relegated to a very unimpressive back room, by no means befitting his rank or his self-esteem. Oster asserted his pride and his character by posting on the wall an old Serbian proverb, "An eagle does not eat flies." He, Hans Oster, had been born an eagle, to soar high in the sky, with the courage of an eagle, and in the end to be downed like an eagle.

Like many patriotic young Germans, Oster had originally felt attracted to the new national-socialist movement, but soon after Hitler's advent to power his attraction turned to aversion, not from democratic conviction, but from monarchist, Christian, and moral principles. Despite this attitude, he was soon appointed Head of the Central Division of Counterintelligence. In this post he acted as Chief-of-Staff and first collaborator of the mysterious Admiral Wilhelm Canaris, head of the Abwehr. As such, Oster was integrated into the O.K.W. (Oberkommando der Wehrmacht), the Supreme Command of the Armed Forces, and was kept informed of the O.K.W.'s plans.

Much has been written about the remarkable Admiral Canaris, determined opponent of the Nazi regime and protector of the resistance movement. He used his high position, which placed him above all suspicion, to plot against the regime, or rather to cover others who did so. His role was in the background, not in active resistance. The fighter's part he was inclined to leave to his trusted deputy Hans Oster, a man of action, who was only too eager to use the free hand thus allowed to him.

What induced Colonel Oster to actions which, as he well knew, would be considered treasonous by many? He acted from deep conviction that in Hitler a dangerous maniac had taken power; if not stopped, this maniac would lead Europe, and Germany itself, to complete ruin. Oster had seen Hitler's methods. For example, on June 30, 1934, Hitler had resolved a sharpening power struggle between the SA and the SS by inventing a fictitious attempted coup d'état by the SA and having its main leaders ruthlessly butchered. Oster resented even more the elimination of General Werner von Fritsch in February 1938 on a false accusation of homosexuality. These and many equally disgusting occurrences had led Oster to conclude that a coup to oust Hitler was the only way to save Germany.*

* Herman Gramml, "Der Fall Oster," *Vierteljahrhefte fuer Zeitgeschichte*, 1966, p. 33.

He did not stop with a theoretical conclusion. His commitment is proven by a concrete plan drawn up in 1938 to capture Hitler in his Chancellery, a plan which failed by pure accident. Oster was active in all subsequent plots to liquidate Hitler.

In addition he took indirect action, trying to prevent an offensive on the Western front, including neutral Holland, Belgium, and Luxemburg, by warning the victims in advance. He hoped that even if the attack were not prevented, his warnings might produce defensive measures that would stop the German offensive. Hence his attempt in April 1940 to warn the British through Sas about the impending operation against Norway and his harping on the destruction of the Meuse bridges at the outset of an attack on the Low Countries.

Whether Colonel Oster committed treason is still very controversial, especially in German military circles. Strictly speaking, he did, for he betrayed his country's vital secrets to the potential enemy. But clearly he was not a traitor in the moral sense. He did not betray his country's interests for financial gain or personal motives. Colonel Oster realized that most of his colleagues, judging by traditional military standards, would condemn his acts. But he was convinced that there are crucial moments in the history of a nation when higher standards may render disobedience—even the betrayal of secrets—a moral obligation.

Oster felt certain that the offensive in the West would not only mean catastrophe for Holland and Belgium, but would ultimately lead to the downfall of Germany itself. Hence preventing the offensive by all possible means became a patriotic duty. He acted accordingly, knowing that he risked his life. History has supported his prophecy about Germany's downfall. And since he paid for his actions with his life, his moral stand cannot be questioned. The borderline between treason and moral resistance is often difficult to distinguish. Colonel Oster acted as Prince Yusupov did when he murdered Rasputin, and as Count Stauffenberg did in his attempt on Hitler's life on July 20, 1944. He has thus taken his place of honour amongst those martyrs of history who sacrificed their lives to free their fatherland from a disastrous ruler.

The eagle's last flight

Although the Gestapo had long suspected Colonel Oster of "treacherous activity" they apparently lacked the evidence and the power over the Abwehr to tackle him; he was even promoted to Major-General. Not until April 5, 1943 did the Gestapo act, and then only indirectly. A sudden investigation was made of his co-conspirator Hans von Dohnanyi, who was arrested in his office. During the search Oster was caught in the act of destroying some incriminating papers; he was temporarily suspended and later relieved of his duties at the Abwehr as of December 31, 1943. His chief, Admiral Canaris, soon received the same treatment, and in February 1944 the whole counterintelligence organization was transferred to the *Reichssicherheithauptamt* (yes, all one word!) of the SS. Canaris and Oster remained provisionally free, but, of course, under close surveillance.

Only after the abortive attempt on Hitler's life on

July 20, 1944 did the Gestapo feel free to proceed against Oster. On July 21 he was arrested and imprisoned in a basement cell in the Gestapo headquarters in the Prinz Albrechtstrasse with Admiral Canaris and several other resistance leaders, including Dr. Hjalmar Schacht, Dr. Joseph Mueller, and Hans von Dohnanyi. After the headquarters was hit by an Allied bombardment on February 3, 1945 these prisoners were transferred to the central bunker of the Flossenburg concentration camp, not far from the Czech border.

Also imprisoned in this solid brick building was Hans Lunding, former chief of the Danish Military Intelligence Service and Lieutenant Colonel of the Danish General Staff. To him we owe the account of the resistance leaders' last months.* The door of Lunding's cell, 21, had a wide crack through which he could look into the corridor; through a window in the opposite wall of the corridor he could also see what happened in the courtyard. To be interrogated and later to be executed, the prisoners were led from the "writing room," about seven meters to the left, past the door of cell 21 to the courtyard. There, just outside Colonel Lunding's view, six rings were fixed to the wall under the eaves. Through these rings were six nooses by which the condemned were usually hanged. Next to the rings a bulletproof lead sheet measuring about one square meter was attached to

* Report of Lieutenant Colonel Hans M. Lunding; K. H. Abshagen, *Canaris* (Stuttgart: Union, 1955) p. 378 ff; Roger Manvell and Heinrich Fraenkel, *The Canaris Conspiracy* (New York: Pinnacle, 1969), pp. 268–270; André Brissaud, *Canaris* (Paris: Librairie Académique Perrin, 1970) pp. 17–29; Hoehne, *Canaris*, p. 569.

the wall. Those selected for the special privilege of being shot in the neck were forced to kneel before the lead sheet.

Admiral Canaris was put in Cell 22. He and Lunding communicated through the common prison system of Morse signals tapped on the wall, and gradually a friendship in the face of death developed between them. Through these messages we know not only what happened to Canaris, but also to Oster, who was imprisoned a few cells farther on.

According to Colonel Lunding, the prisoners were not physically tortured during the first weeks, although they were constantly interrogated in the most tormenting way. The prisoners, knowing that they would be condemned, tried to drag out the interrogation until the approaching American forces could liberate the camp. At the end of March Ernst Kaltenbrunner, head of the Gestapo and Canaris' archenemy, came to the camp himself to interrogate his old enemy. Only after that visit did the Gestapo start to torture the prisoners physically.

Kaltenbrunner also directed that the resistance leaders among the inmates should be liquidated; they knew too much. However, even in those last weeks the Nazis adhered strictly to the *Fuehrerprinzip*, the principle that the Fuehrer should always make the final decision, and to the semblance of legality. On April 5, in the bunker under the ruins of the Reichskanzlei in Berlin, surrounded by Russian troops and under a hail of artillery shells, Hitler himself decided that Canaris, Oster, Dohnanyi, and a few others should be hanged. The sentence should formally be pronounced by a "summary court" in the camp. It should be justified by the diaries and notebooks of Admiral Canaris, which were found by pure chance early in 1945 in a safe at headquarters in Zossen. On April 6 these diaries were turned over to Kaltenbrunner, who then ordered the execution of the conspirators.*

On Sunday, April 8, the "summary court" was held in the concentration camp. This travesty was performed by the SS. Oster was the first accused. He pleaded guilty to conspiring to overthrow Hitler but not to assassinate him.

Until late that night the SS tried to obtain full confessions from the accused, but these held out steadfastly. The "summary court" then condemned Admiral Canaris, Oster, the Rev. Dietrich Bonhoeffer, Dr. Karl Sack, and two other resistance companions to death.

When Admiral Canaris returned to his cell that night after an hour-long "pressing interrogation," he informed his next-door neighbor in Morse signals that he had been severely maltreated and his nose had been broken. He was now convinced that he and his five companions would be put to death.

When?

Tomorrow at dawn.

He then tapped his last message: "I die for my country; my conscience is clear. You as an officer must understand that I only did my patriotic duty when I tried to rebel against the criminal madness with which Hitler is

* Brissaud, *Canaris*, p. 330.

leading Germany to disaster. It was useless, because I now know that this Germany will perish."

We cannot know Oster's thoughts during the last hours of his life. Probably they were much like those of Canaris, for he had said as much to his son about two years earlier, as the son told me later. Undoubtedly he felt that his acts had been justified, for his prediction about Germany's fate was now being fulfilled. As a religious man he would have accounted for his deeds to God, whose judgment was far more important to him than that of an SS court. Perhaps he also remembered what he once said to a friend: "It is much easier to take a pistol and shoot someone to pieces, or even to walk into machine gun fire, than to do what I have decided to do. If ever you should get into that position I beg of you: even after my death remain my friend and understand what has induced me to do things which others may never understand, or would at least never have done themselves."

Toward six in the morning the barking of dogs indicated that people were busy in the courtyard. Dawn was just breaking but harsh floodlights lit the site of the execution. The steps of heavy jackboots, clanging doors, swearing, and coarse orders awakened the prisoners. Lunding could hear as some of the condemned were dragged from their cells.

"Cell 22!"

A key ground in the lock; the hinges of the cell door creaked and groaned.

"Out with you!"

Once the prisoners were outside their cells, their wrist and leg irons were taken off and fell clattering on the stone floor. The men were taken to the writing room on the left. Someone shouted, "Undress! Everything off!"

The condemned knew what this meant; the SS always executed its victims naked.

"Go!"

The silent witness in Cell 21 saw the naked upper part of a small man with gray hair, a battered face, and piercing blue eyes shuffle past the window. It was Admiral Canaris. Lunding could not see the execution itself. He waited, wondering whether he would hear a shot. A German officer was entitled to die only by the bullet, an old tradition which was usually respected even by the SS.

Not this time. No shot resounded. That meant the piano-wire noose. From the scaffold a voice barked:

"Next!"

and from the writing room someone roared:

"Go!"

Again a naked, emaciated, and battered man, but with his head held high, shuffled past the window on the courtyard. Colonel Oster, humiliated, beaten, tortured, but unbroken in spirit, moved through the pale light of dawn to the floodlit scaffold to meet his Creator.

For a few moments there was no sound. Then the voice on the right barked again:

"Next!"

and the voice from the left:
"Go!"

Six times the orders from left and right resounded.
Then there was silence, the silence that would be eternal
for the victims.

A short while later their fellow prisoner and friend,
Dr. Josef Mueller, smelled the nauseating odor of burning human flesh. He rushed to the cell window and
nearly fainted when he saw, rising from the crema-
torium, small scorched flakes of human skin, the skin of
his friends, being blown through the bars into his cell.*

Fate played its last irony: the executions took place
on April 9, at the break of dawn—five years to the day
since, also at the break of dawn, the Nazis had invaded
Denmark and Norway. This invasion and its aftermath
Oster had tried to prevent in his attempt to save his own
country. Even as he died for his belief, his prophecy was
being fulfilled.

A few days later Flossenburg concentration camp was
liberated by the American forces. But the fall of the
Third Reich came too late to save Oster. The eagle who
despised flies had taken off on his last and highest flight,
the flight from which there is no return.

* Harold Deutsch, *Verschwoerung gegen den Krieg* (Munich Beck-Verlag,
1969), p. 388; Manvell and Fraenkel, *Canaris Conspiracy*, p. 269; Hoehne,
Canaris, p. 569.

BIBLIOGRAPHY

(Titles in original language)

Abshagen, K. H. *Canaris. Stuttgart: Union*, 1955.

Andenaes, Johs; Riste, Olav; and Skodvin, Magne. *Norway and the Second World War*. Oslo: Johand Grundt Tanum Forlag, 1966.

Best, S. Payne. *The Venlo Incident*. London: Hutchinson, 1950.

Brissaud, André. *Canaris, le petit amiral, prince de l'espionage allemand*. Paris: Librairie Académique Perrin, 1970.

Brodersen, Prof. Arvid. *"Et Varsel fra Berlin." Farmand*, No. 8, February 25, 1978.

Buchheit, Gert. *Der deutsche Geheimdienst. Geschichte der militaerischen Abwehr*. Munich 1966.

Burckhardt, Carl Jacob. *Meine Danziger Mission 1937–1939*. Zurich: Fretz und Wasmuth, 1960.

Davignon, Vicomte Jacques, *Berlin 1939–1940*. Paris-Bruxelles: Ed. Universitaires, 1951.

Deutsch, Prof. Harold. *Verschwoerung gegen den Krieg*. Munich: Beck Verlag, 1969.

Gisevius, Hans B. *Bis zum bitteren Ende*. Zurich: Fretz und Wasmuth, 1946. Reprint Frankfurt-Berlin: Ullstein

Buecher, 1964. English trans. Boston: Houghton Mifflin, 1947.

Gramml, Hermann. *"Der Fall Oster." Vierteljahrhefte fuer Zeitgeschichte* 14, 1966, pp. 26–39.

Groscurth, Helmuth. *Tagebuecher eines Abwehrofficiers, 1938–1940*. Stuttgart: Deutsche Verlagsanstalt.

Halder, Generaloberst. *Kriegstagebuch Band I: Vom Polenfeldzug bis zum Ende der Westoffensive*. Stuttgart: Kohlhammer Verlag, 1962.

Hoffmann, Peter. *Widerstand, Staatsstreich, Attentat*. Munich: Piper und Co. English trans. Cambridge, MA: MIT. Press, 1976.

Höhne, Heinz. *Canaris, Patriot im Zwielicht*. Munich: Bertelsmann Verlag, 1976.

Innstilling fra Undersøkelsescommission av 1945 [Report of the Norwegian Parliamentary Commission of Inquiry of 1945]. Oslo: the Storting [Norwegian Parliament], 1946.

Jacobson, Hans-Adolf. *Dokumente zur Vorgeschichte des Westfeldzuges 1939–49*. Berlin-Frankfurt 1956.

———. *Fall Gelb: Der Kampf um den deutschen Operationsplan zur Westoffensive 1940*. Wiesbaden: Franz Steiner Verlag, 1957.

———. *Kriegstagebuch des Oberkommandos der Wehrmacht (Wehrmachtfuehrungsstab)*, vol. I, August 1940–December 31, 1941. Frankfurt 1965.

Jong, Dr. L. de. *"Het Koninkrijk der Nederlanden in de Tweede Wereldoorlog. Neutraal*, vol. 2.

Kjølsen, Admiral F. H. *"Advarslerne fra Berlin før den 9. April 1940."* Saertryk of Politikens Kronik, March 31, 1965.

———. *Optakten til den 9. April*, Copenhagen 1945.

Kleffens, E. N. van. *The Rape of the Netherlands*. London: Hodder and Stoughton, 1940.

Koeltz, Général Louis. *Comment s'est joué notre destin–Hitler et l'offensive de 10 mai 1940*. Paris: Librairie Hachette, 1957.

Kordt, Erich. *Nicht aus den Akten*. Stuttgart: Union, 1950.

Manvell R., and Fraenkel, H. *The Canaris Conspiracy*. New York: Pinnacle Books, 1969.

Norden, Peter. *Salon Kitty, Ein Report*. Munich: Suedwest Verlag, 1970.

Parlementaire Enquetecommissie Regeringsbeleid, 1940–1945. [Netherlands Parliamentary Commission of Inquiry of Government Policy 1940–1945], vols. I, a, b, and c: Neutrality policy; Departure of the Government; First Months in London. Especially relevant:
Vol. 1. The Attitude of Headquarters in view of the German Invasion, p. 109.
Vol. 2a. Events immediately preceding May 10, 1940, p. 60.
Vol. 2c. Testimony of Maj. Gen. G. J. Sas, p. 207.
Vol. 2c. Testimony of Mr. E. N. van Kleffens, p. 285.
Vol. 2c. Testimony of Dr. J. G. de Beus, p. 557.

Pearson, Fred. S., and Doerga, R. E. "*Small States and Foreign Policy Crisis; the Netherlands and the 1940 Nazi Invasion*," October 1977.

"*Polnische Dokumente zur Vorgeschichte des Krieges.*" Basel 1940.

Roon, Dr. Ger van. "*Oberst Wilhelm Stachle; ein Beitrag zu den Auslandskontakten des deutschen Widerstandes.*" V. *fuer Zeitgeschichte* 14 (1966), pp. 209–233.

————. *Der Kreisauer Kreis innerhalb der deutschen Widerstandsbewegung*. Munich, 1967.

Sas, Bert. "*Het begon in Mei 1940.*" *De Spiegel*, October 4 and 7, 1953.

Sendtner, Kurt. *"Die deutsche Militaeropposition im ersten Kriegsjahr." Vollmacht des Gewissens I.* Frankfurt-Berlin: Eur. Publikationen, 1960, pp. 385–532.

Somer, Dr. J. M. *"Report on events at General Headquarters during the days preceding the German Invasion,"* London, April 2, 1943.

Standaardgeschiedenis van de Tweede Wereldoorlog, under supervision of Sir Basil Liddell Hart. Antwerp: Standaard, 1968.

Welkenhuyzen, Jean van. *"Het Alarm van Januari 1940 in Nederland." Bijdragen tot de Geschiedenis van de Tweede Wereldoorlog,* pp. 127 ff.

———. *"Les Avertissements qui venaient de Berlin."* Unpublished manuscript.

INDEX OF NAMES

(With positions held in 1939–1940)

Abs, Dr. Hermann, Director of the Reichsbank, 140, 143
Auer, Counselor of Legation in the German Foreign Office,
    128
Beaverbrook, Lord, newspaper magnate, 134
Beck, General Ludwig, former Chief of the German General
    Staff, 55
Bernstorff, Count Albrecht von, ousted from the German
    diplomatic service by the Nazis, 74
Berryer, Vicomte J. de, Counselor of the Belgian Embassy in
    Berlin, 122–25, 128
Best, Captain Payne, Head of the Passport Division of the
    British Legation in The Hague, 63–65
Bismarck, Prince Otto von, Minister Plenipotentiary and Head
    of the Political Division in the German Foreign
    Office, 65
Bland, Sir Neville, British Minister in The Hague, 59, 108
Boetzelaer, Baron C. G. W. H. van tot Oosterhout, Counselor
    of the Netherlands Legation in Berlin until March
    1940, 100, 127
Bonhoeffer, Rev. Dietrich, German resistance leader, 176
Bosch, Jonkheer Herbert van Drakesteyn, Counselor of the

Netherlands Legation in Berlin from April 1940, 127, 129, 132, 150–51

Braeuer, Dr. Curt, German Minister in Oslo, 100–1, 104–5

Brauchitsch, General Walther von, German Commander-in-Chief, 56

Burckhardt, Carl Jacob, High Commissioner of the League of Nations in the Free City of Danzig, 25, 34–38

Canaris, Admiral Wilhelm, Head of the German Counterintelligence Service, 120, 159, 171, 173–78

Chodacki, Minister, Polish Representative to the Free City of Danzig, 33, 35

Chamberlain, Sir Neville, British Prime Minister, 136

Churchill, Sir Winston, British Prime Minister 1940, 98, 134

Cochran, Merle, American diplomat, 31–32

Colijn, Dr. Hendrik C., former Prime Minister of the Netherlands, 59–60, 68

Constantinides, Greek Military Attaché in Berlin, 121

Coulondre, Robert, French Ambassador in Berlin, 30, 158

Davies, Liberal English member of Parliament, 134

Davignon, Vicomte Jacques, Belgian Ambassador in Berlin, 49–51

Dickens, Vice Admiral Sir Gerald C., British Naval Attaché at The Hague, 108

Dyxhoorn, General, Netherlands Minister of Defense, 145

Dohnanyi, Hans von, resistance leader, 173–75

Dollfuss, Engelbert, Chancellor of Austria, 17

Doernberg, Freiherr von, Chief of Protocol at the German Foreign Office, 155

Eberhardt, General, Police Commander in Danzig, 34

Forshell, Anders, Swedish Naval Attache in Berlin, 105

Forster, Gauleiter of the National-Socialist Party in Danzig, 25, 35, 38

Francois-Poncet, André, French Ambassador in Berlin until 1938, 76

Frank, Hans, Nazi Governor-General of the General Government Poland, 42

Gamelin, General Maurice G., French Commander-in-Chief, 83, 136

Gaus, Undersecretary of State in the German Foreign Office, 128, 147

Gevers, Baron W. J. G., Chargé d'affaires a.i. of the Netherlands Legation in Warsaw, 25

Gisevius, Hans Bernd, official of the German Ministry of the Interior, 69

Goebbels, Nazi Minister of Propaganda, 62

Goering, Field Marshal Hermann, German Minister for Air, 69, 87, 132–33, 165, 167–68

Goethals, Col. Georges, Belgian Military Attaché in Berlin, 48–50, 71, 97, 119, 123, 128

Greiser, Arthur, President of the Senate of the Free City of Danzig, 34–35

Groscurth, Liaison Officer of the German Counterintelligence at Headquarters in Zossen, 55

Haakon, King of Norway, 114

Haersma de With, Jonkheer H. M. van, Minister in Berlin, 16, 23, 51, 55–56, 64, 73–75, 97, 141, 145, 147–49

Halder, General Franz, Chief of the German General Staff, 48, 50, 55, 87, 114, 170

Halem, von, Counselor of Legation, Deputy Chief of Protocol in the German Foreign Office, 150–51

Harinxma Thoe Slooten, Baron van, Netherlands Ambassador in Brussels, 131

Heath, Donald, First Secretary in the U.S. Embassy in Berlin, 31–32, 44, 136, 140, 143–44

Helfrich, Staatsrat, President of German-Netherlands Society, Berlin, 29

Henderson, Sir Neville, British Ambassador in Berlin, 30

Hewel, Counselor of Legation and Personal Aide to Hitler, 93–94

Hitler, Adolf, German dictator, 14–15, 17–21, 24, 29, 30, 34–35, 40–41, 46, 53, 55–56, 62, 64, 66–67, 69, 70, 73, 76, 78, 80, 85–89, 93, 95, 102, 109, 110, 112–14, 118, 132–33, 151, 172, 175–76

Horstmann, Freddie, former German diplomat and host in Berlin, 136

Ironside, General Sir Edmund, British Commander-in-Chief, 110

Jodl, General Alfred, Hitler's Personal Chief of Staff, 73, 87, 118

Kaltenbrunner, Ernst, head of the Gestapo, 175–76

Keitel, General Field Marshal Wilhelm, 30, 69, 87, 119

Kiewitz, Major Werner, special envoy of Hitler, 126, 130–33, 146

Kirk, Alexander, U.S. Chargé d'affaires in Berlin, 31–32, 140, 144

Kjølsen, F. H., Danish Naval Attaché in Berlin, 105–7

Kleikamp, Capt. Wilhelm, Commander of the "Schleswig-Holstein," 33–34, 38

Kleffens, Dr. Eelco van, Netherlands Minister for Foreign Affairs, 61, 76, 108, 145

Klop, Lieutenant of the Netherlands General Staff, 63–65

Koht, Halvdan, Norwegian Minister for Foreign Affairs, 98, 103

Kuehlmann, Richard von, German diplomat, 126

Kuykendall, U.S. Consul General in Danzig, 26

Leopold III, King of the Belgians, 61, 69, 149

Limburg Stirum, Count van, Netherlands Ambassador in Berlin in 1936, 23

Lunding, Col. Hans M., former Chief of the Danish Military Intelligence Service, 174–75, 177–78

Luns, Joseph M. A. H., Attaché at the Netherlands Legation in Bern, 162

Maasdijk, "Jerry" van, correspondent of *De Telegraaf* in Berlin, 74

Maessen de Sombreff, Jonkheer van der, Netherlands honorary Consul-General in Danzig, 24

Maglione, Cardinal Luigi, Secretary of State in the Vatican, 120

Michiels van Verduynen, Jonkheer F., Netherlands Ambassador in London, 134–35

Moderow, Polish member of the Harbor Commission of Danzig, 27

Molotov, V., Minister for Foreign Affairs of the U.S.S.R., 29

Moolenburgh, Naval Lieutenant, Liaison officer in the Dept. of Defense, 108

Morgenthau, Henry, U.S. Secretary of the Treasury, 31–32

Mueller, Dr. Josef, representative of the Canaris resistance group, 120, 174, 179

Munch, Edvard, Danish Minister for Foreign Affairs, 106

Oster, Col. Hans, Head of the Central Section in the German Counterintelligence Service, 169–75, 178–79

Plassche, Lt. Col. van de, Chief of GS III in Netherlands Ministry of Defense, 141–42

Pohlman, courier of Auswaertige Amt, 104

Post Uyterweer, Naval Lieutenant, Aide de Camp to Dutch Minister for Defense, 139–40

Quisling, Vidkun, former Norwegian Minister of Defense and Head of Norwegian Nazi movement, 101–2

Raeder, Grossadmiral Erich, Commander-in-Chief German Navy, 102, 110

Raeder, Gudrun, official in Norwegian Foreign Office, 103

Reigenberger, Major Helmuth, paratroop officer, 83

Reynders, General, Netherlands Commander-in-Chief, 47, 54, 58, 60, 78, 83–85

Reimke, Hofrat, in German Foreign Office, 126–28, 130

Ribbentrop, Joachim von, German Minister for Foreign Affairs, 29, 76, 81, 94, 112, 113, 125, 128, 131–33, 136, 146–48, 150

Rijkens, Paul, President of Unilever concern, 134–35

Rintelen, Dr. E. von, Counselor of Legation in German Foreign Office, 92–93, 124–26

Roijen, Dr. J. H. van, Director of Political Affairs in Netherlands Foreign Office, 108, 127, 128

Roosevelt, Franklin D., President of U.S., 143–44

Sack, Dr. Karl, German lawyer who defended victims of Nazi prosecution, 176

Sas, Major Gijsbert J., Military Attaché in Netherlands Legation, Berlin, 21, 45–61, 67–76, 78, 80, 85, 87, 89, 95–100, 103, 105–7, 109, 111, 113–17, 119, 121–24, 128, 133, 135, 138–39, 141–43, 151, 154, 159, 165–69, 172

Schacht, Dr. Hjalmar, German Minister for Finance, 31, 174

Scheel, A., Norwegian Minister in Berlin, 99–100, 102

Schlieffen, General von, author of a 1911 German western offensive plan, 47

Schmieden, Dr. von, official of German Foreign Office, 128

Schoen, Secretary of the Danish Legation in Berlin, 107

Schrader, Commander Werner, Naval Attaché of the U.S. Embassy in Berlin, 107

Soltikov, Count Michael, official of the German Counterintelligence Service, 159

Spaak, Paul-Henri, Belgian Minister for Foreign Affairs, 85

Stang, Ulrich, Counselor of the Norwegian Legation in Berlin, pp. 97–100, 102–3, 105

Stauffenberg, Count von, attempted to kill Hitler July 20, 1944, 173

Stevens, Major R. H., agent of the British Intelligence Service, 63, 65

Tippelskirch, General Werner von, German Quartermaster General, 48, 50

Todt, Fritz, main architect of the Third Reich, 126

Wagner, Counselor of Legation in German Foreign Office, 146

Wegener, Wolfgang, author of *The Naval Strategy of the World War*, 110

Weiszaecker, Ernst, Freiherr von, State Secretary in the German Foreign Office, 126

Welkenhuyzen, Jean van, Director of the Belgian Research Center for the History of World War II, 10

Wilhelmina, Queen of the Netherlands, 60–61, 69, 130, 132, 149, 166

Witzleben, General von, German Commander at the western front, 58

Woermann, Dr. Ernst, State Secretary in the German Foreign Office, 94, 126

Zahle, Kammerherre, Danish Minister in Berlin, 106–7

Zapp, German Counselor of Legation, 156–7